Resource Financed Infrastructure

A WORLD BANK STUDY

Resource Financed Infrastructure

A Discussion on a New Form of Infrastructure Financing

Håvard Halland, John Beardsworth, Bryan Land, and James Schmidt

With comments by
Paul Collier
Alan Gelb
Justin Yifu Lin and Yan Wang
Clare Short
Louis Wells

THE WORLD BANK
Washington, D.C.

HUNTON&
WILLIAMS

PPIAF
Enabling Infrastructure Investment

ISBN (paper): 978-1-4648-0239-3
ISBN (electronic): 978-1-4648-0240-9
DOI: 10.1596/978-1-4648-0239-3

Cover photo: Getty Images / Sam Edwards. Used with permission; further permission required for reuse.
Cover design: Debra Naylor, Naylor Design Inc.

Library of Congress Cataloging-in-Publication Data has been requested.

Contents

Boxes

Figures

Tables

Acknowledgments

This report was prepared under the guidance of Håvard Halland, natural resource economist, and Bryan C. Land, lead mining specialist, both of the World Bank. It centers on a study by consultants to the Bank: John J. Beardsworth, Jr., partner and global head, and James A. Schmidt, counsel, both of Hunton & Williams LLP. Comments by Paul Collier, Alan Gelb, Justin Yifu Lin and Yan Wang, Clare Short, and Louis T. Wells have enormously enriched the debate that this report represents.

The editors are extremely grateful to the global experts who helped hone the initial concept for this work: Paul Collier, Shanta Devarajan, and Deborah Brautigam. Several people provided highly useful feedback on earlier drafts, including Pierre A. Pozzo di Borgo, Nicola Smithers, Marijn Verhoeven, and James Close, and—on the concept note—Xavier Cledan Mandri-Perrott, Anand Rajaram, Nadir Mohammed, Jyoti Bisbey, and Tomoko Matsukawa. Otaviano Canuto provided critical advice at various stages of the work process, and Vivien Foster at the initial stage. Timely research assistance was provided by Mariela Sánchez Martiarena, and copyediting by Fayre Makeig. The report would not have been possible without invaluable managerial support from William Dorotinsky and Nick Manning.

Finally, the World Bank would like to acknowledge financial contributions from the Department of Foreign Affairs and Trade of the Government of Australia, which is supporting the Bank's research program on extractive industries in Africa, and from the Public-Private Infrastructure Advisory Facility. All opinions, errors, and omissions are the authors' own.

About the Authors

Håvard Halland is a natural resource economist at the World Bank, where he leads research and policy agendas in the fields of resource-backed infrastructure finance, sovereign wealth fund policy, extractives revenue management, and public financial management for the extractives sector. Prior to joining the World Bank, he was a delegate and program manager for the International Committee of the Red Cross (ICRC) in the Democratic Republic of the Congo and Colombia. He holds a PhD in economics from the University of Cambridge.

John J. Beardsworth, Jr., is head of the business practice group of the international law firm Hunton & Williams LLP and a member of the firm's Executive Committee. With more than 30 years of experience, he focuses his practice on resource development, energy and infrastructure transactions, and project finance. Mr. Beardsworth has extensive experience in restructuring and privatizing infrastructure enterprises, and in the development, financing, and construction of resource- and infrastructure-related assets. He is recognized for his long-standing practice in Africa. Mr. Beardsworth earned a JD with honors from The George Washington University Law School in 1979 and a BA from the University of Pennsylvania, magna cum laude, in 1975.

Bryan C. Land is a lead mining specialist at the World Bank and has been developing the Bank's research into the opportunities and challenges faced by resource-rich African countries. Prior to joining the World Bank, Mr. Land led the Commonwealth Secretariat's program on natural resource management. Previously he was at extractive industry consulting houses IHS Energy and CRU International and also spent three years in Papua New Guinea in the Department of Minerals and Energy. Mr. Land earned a bachelor's degree in economics from the London School of Economics and master's degrees in international affairs and natural resources law from Columbia University and Dundee University, respectively.

James A. Schmidt is counsel with the international law firm of Hunton & Williams LLP. With more than 25 years of experience, Mr. Schmidt focuses on electric sector restructuring and market design, creating legislative and regulatory frameworks, developing independent regulatory agencies, and negotiating infrastructure projects for private developers, governments and their utilities, and public-private partnerships. He served as lead attorney for energy and regulatory reform matters in the legal department of the World Bank between 1996 and 1998. He was also a law clerk for the U.S. Court of Appeals for the Fourth Circuit between 1986 and 1989. Mr. Schmidt earned a JD from the University of Wisconsin Law School in 1986 and a BA from Lawrence University in 1983.

About the Commentators

Paul Collier is a professor of economics and public policy at the Blavatnik School of Government, a professorial fellow of St. Antony's College, and codirector of the Centre for the Study of African Economies, Oxford. From 1998 to 2003, he was director of the Research Development Department of the World Bank. He is currently a *professeur invité* at Sciences Po, and at Paris 1. Professor Collier is an adviser to the Strategy and Policy Department of the International Monetary Fund, to the Africa Region of the World Bank, and to the United Kingdom's Department for International Development (DfID). He has written for the *New York Times*, the *Financial Times*, the *Wall Street Journal*, and the *Washington Post*, and is the author of several books. In 2008, Professor Collier received a knighthood for services to promote research and policy change in Africa.

Alan Gelb is a senior fellow at the Center for Global Development. He was previously with the World Bank in a number of positions, including director of development policy and chief economist for the Africa region. His research areas include the management of resource-rich economies, African economic development, results-based financing, and the use of digital identification technology for development. He has written a number of books and papers in scholarly journals. He earned a B.Sc. in applied mathematics from the University of Natal and a B.Phil. and D.Phil. from Oxford University.

Justin Yifu Lin is professor and honorary dean, National School of Development at Peking University, and councilor of the State Council. He was the senior vice president and chief economist of the World Bank, 2008–12. Prior to this, Mr. Lin served for 15 years as founding director and professor of the China Centre for Economic Research (CCER) at Peking University. He is the author of 23 books, including *New Structural Economics: A Framework for Rethinking Development and Policy*. He is a member of the Standing Committee, Chinese People's Political Consultation Conference, and vice chairman of the All-China Federation of Industry and Commerce. He is a corresponding fellow of the British Academy and a fellow of the Academy of Sciences for the Developing World.

Clare Short is the chair of the EITI Board, elected at the EITI Global Conference in Paris in March 2011. The Rt. Hon. Clare Short was previously the UK Secretary of State for International Development (1997–2003). As the first person to hold this position, she played a key role in elevating the United Kingdom's profile and budget for sustainable development and poverty elimination. Ms. Short entered the House of Commons in 1983 as the member of Parliament for her native Birmingham Ladywood. She was shadow minister for women (1993–95), shadow secretary of state for transport (1995–96), and opposition spokesperson on overseas development (1996–97). Ms. Short is a member of the Advisory Committee of International Lawyers for Africa and a trustee of Africa Humanitarian Action.

Yan Wang is a senior visiting fellow at the National School of Development, Peking University, and a visiting professor at the School of Business, George Washington University. Previously she worked as senior economist and team leader in the World Bank for 20 years and gained in-depth experience working with governments and the private sector in emerging market economies. She also served as coordinator of the Organisation for Economic Co-operation and Development (OECD) Development Assistance Committee (DAC) and China Study Group for two years (2009–11), working on China-Africa development cooperation and investment. She has authored and coauthored several books and journal publications and received the SUN Yefang Award in Economics. She received her PhD from Cornell University, and taught economics before joining the World Bank.

Louis T. Wells is the Herbert F. Johnson Professor of International Management, emeritus, at the Harvard Business School. He has served as a consultant to governments of a number of developing countries, as well as to international organizations and private firms. His principal consulting activities and publications have been concerned with foreign investment policy, negotiations between foreign investors and host governments, and settlement of investment disputes. He was the coordinator for Indonesia Projects, Harvard Institute for International Development, Jakarta, in 1994–95. Professor Wells received a BS in physics from Georgia Tech and his MBA and DBA from the Harvard Business School.

Abbreviations

CFR	collaterization of future revenues
EITI	Extractive Industries Transparency Initiative
EPC	engineering, procurement, and construction
FDI	foreign direct investment
FIDIC	International Federation of Consulting Engineers
GDP	gross domestic product
GSTF	Global Structural Transformation Fund
IBRD	International Bank for Reconstruction and Development
ICT	information and communication technology
IEEE	Institute of Electrical and Electronics Engineers
IFI	international finance institution
IMF	International Monetary Fund
IPP	independent power project
LDCs	less developed countries
MDB	multilateral development bank
MOU	memorandum of understanding
NGO	nongovernmental organization
O&M	operations and maintenance
PIU	project implementation unit
PPP	public-private partnership
RAF	revenue anticipation financing
RfI	resources for infrastructure
RFI	resource financed infrastructure
SPV	special purpose vehicle
SWOT	strengths, weaknesses, opportunities, threats
UNCTAD	United Nations Conference on Trade and Development

PART 1

Key Perspectives

Håvard Halland

Overview

Scope and Focus

This report, consisting of a study prepared by global project finance specialists Hunton & Williams LLP and comments from six internationally reputed economists and policy makers, provides an analytical discussion of resource financed infrastructure (RFI) contracting from a project finance perspective. The report is meant as a forum for in-depth discussion and as a basis for further research into RFI's role, risks, and potential, without any intention to present a World Bank–supported view on RFI contracting. It is motivated by the conviction that if countries are to continue to either seek RFI or receive unsolicited RFI proposals, there is an onus on public officials to discern bad deals from good, to judge unavoidable trade-offs, and to act accordingly. The report aims to provide a basis for developing insights on how RFI deals can be made subject to the same degree of public policy scrutiny as any other instrument through which a government of a low- or lower-middle-income country might seek to mobilize development finance.

The report also feeds into the global mainstreaming of "open contracting," providing citizens with the means to engage with governments and other stakeholders on how nonrenewable resources are best managed for the public benefit. In the case of RFI, there is a very direct link made between the value of resources in the ground and the development of (infrastructure) benefits. It should not be a surprise, therefore, that the revised Extractive Industries Transparency Initiative (EITI) Standard, adopted in May 2013, addresses extractive transactions with an infrastructure component, including RFI.[1]

To undertake the study, the World Bank asked John Beardsworth, Jr., and James Schmidt of global project finance specialist Hunton & Williams LLP to analyze the RFI model from a structural, legal, financial, and operational perspective. Topics include the model's financing characteristics; the valuation of RFI exchanges; the model's relationship to a given fiscal regime; sharing of risks and liabilities; settlement of disputes; construction supervision arrangements; specification of technical standards; as well as operations and maintenance. The resulting study argues that RFI deals are a derivation of more traditional models of finance (namely, resource concessions, traditional government infrastructure purchases, project finance, and public-private partnerships) and can be bench-marked against these. The study goes on to examine the identity and interests of the parties to RFI deals, the risks assumed, undertakings made, and explores options for safeguards to ensure that the public interest is served.

Given its focus on contractual and financing issues, the study does not address wider contextual issues (such as the appraisal, selection, monitoring, and evalua-tion of infrastructure projects) or macroeconomic and institutional absorption issues arising from increased infrastructure investment. As RFI loans have been predominantly in the form of export credit, with labor and intermediary goods imported from the funding country, potential problems around macroeconomic absorption have been reduced. But the extensive use of imports raises other issues—around local employment, national value added, and contribution to economic diversification. Finally, as noted by Alan Gelb (in "Comments," Part 3 of this report), the study does not address wider debates regarding the collater-alization of future government revenue, and implications for fiscal stability and creditworthiness.[2]

RFI Essentials

Under an RFI arrangement, a loan for current infrastructure construction is secu-ritized against the net present value of a future revenue stream from oil or mineral extraction, adjusted for risk. Loan disbursements for infrastructure con-struction usually start shortly after a joint infrastructure-resource extraction contract is signed, and are paid directly to the construction company to cover construction costs. The revenues for paying down the loan, which are disbursed directly from the oil or mining company to the financing institution, often begin a decade or more later, after initial capital investments for the extractive project have been recovered. The grace period for the infrastructure loan thus depends on how long it takes to build the mine or develop the oil field, on the size of the initial investment, and on its rate of return. Large extractive projects can cost between $3 billion and $15 billion and take 10 years or more from discovery to commercial operation and several more years for initial investments to be recouped. Infrastructure financed through RFI arrangements includes power plants, railways, roads, information and communication technology (ICT) proj-ects, schools and hospitals, and water works (Foster and others 2009; Korea ExIm Bank 2011; Alves 2013).

RFI deals—not to be confused with "packaged" resource-infrastructure deals, in which infrastructure is ancillary to resource extraction (such as rail-to-port links for ore transport)—may be seen as a continuation of oil-backed lending practices pioneered by Standard Chartered Bank, BNP Paribas, Commerzbank, and others in Angola in the 1980s and 1990s (Brautigam 2011). According to

Alves (2013) oil-backed lending remains a common format for several banks that do business in Africa. Louis Wells, in the "Comments" section (Part 3 of this report), argues that signature bonuses, common in the extractive industries sector, are also similar to RFI deals, in the sense that they provide assets now for access to minerals or other natural resources later.

Like oil-backed lending, RFI deals were pioneered in Angola. China ExIm Bank started offering this type of contract in 2004, and RFI later became a main vehicle for financing Angola's postwar reconstruction (Brautigam 2011). The RFI mode of contracting was later used in several other African countries—predominantly by Chinese banks, including China Development Bank, but recently also by Korea Exim Bank for the Musoshi mine project in the Democratic Republic of Congo (DRC). According to Korea Exim Bank (2011), "the [Korean version of the RFI] model was strategically developed to increase Korea's competitiveness against countries which have already advanced into the promising market of Africa. This agreement is the first application of the model." Back-of-the-envelope estimates based on publicly available information indicate the value of signed RFI contracts in Africa to be at least $30 billion, although it is unclear how many of these contracts have been fully implemented. In 2011 and 2012, $6 billion worth of contracts were reportedly signed, with $14 billion in contract value reportedly under negotiation in 2013.[3]

The emergence of the RFI model can be understood, in part, as a reflection of the gap in risk tolerance and expected return between the extractive and the infrastructure sectors. Many developing countries continue to face large financing gaps for public infrastructure, with estimates indicating an annual cost of $93 billion to address Africa's infrastructure needs—more than double the current level (Foster and Briceño-Garmendia 2010). The global financial crisis and its aftermath have dramatically strained the sources of traditional, private, and long-term finance available to developing countries, in particular for infrastructure. In parallel, aid flows have been diminishing. Foreign direct investment (FDI) in the extractives sector, on the other hand, has increased over the past decade in many developing countries. Though the recent softening of mineral commodity prices rules out more marginal mining projects, billion-dollar investments continue to pour into the sector—even under the most difficult geographical and political circumstances, particularly in Africa. As a result, less developed countries (LDCs) have in fact been receiving more FDI—as a share of gross domestic product (GDP)—than other more advanced developing countries (Brahmbhatt and Canuto 2013). FDI to Africa has quintupled since the turn of the millennium, from $10 billion in 2000 to $50 billion in 2012 (UNCTAD 2013). This reflects the fact that many developing countries that lack access to capital markets are also rich in natural resources. Several of these countries have been using their natural resources as collateral to access sources of finance for investment, countervailing barriers to conventional bank lending and capital markets. RFI is one of several contractual arrangements born out of this context.

RFI Debated

Six globally prominent economists and policy makers have commented on this study, providing additional depth, insights, contexts, and perspectives (see "Comments," Part 3 of this report). Several of the commentators argue that RFI—which by conventional principles is undesirable because, among other reasons, it reduces future fiscal flexibility by earmarking funds for infrastructure—might nevertheless be the best option available in contexts with weak public administration capacity and procurement systems. According to Paul Collier, fiscal flexibility need not always be desirable, and earmarking resource revenues for investment could, in context with high spending pressures, be preferable. Like Alan Gelb and Louis Wells, he argues that RFI represents a *commitment mechanism*, enabling ministers responsible for the depletion of natural resource assets to ensure that future decision makers devote a sensible proportion of resource revenues to the accumulation of assets. The government achieves this precommitment by signing away the prospective revenues to finance infrastructure, through an RFI deal, and is thereby better able to resist pressures for increased recurrent spending from resource revenues. Oil-backed lending, on the other hand, does not offer this commitment mechanism.

Justin Yifu Lin, Yan Wang, and Wells contend that committing resource revenues to infrastructure construction through RFI deals may prevent capital flight that may otherwise result from an abundance of resource revenues in a context of weak financial and political institutions. Gelb points to the risk of revenues from extractives either failing to be included in the national budget or, if included, being wasted or stolen, and argues that RFI's inherent precommitment mechanism may reduce such risks. He also sees this mechanism as limiting the ability of a government to raid resource revenues accumulated in a sovereign wealth fund by a more responsible prior government. In more general terms, Lin and Wang argue that RFI could "help overcome severe financial and governance constraints suffered by low-income but resource-rich countries."

Beardsworth and Schmidt contend that one reason that RFI deals may be perceived as attractive for governments is the opportunity that these deals offer to provide returns to citizens while decision makers are still in office, long before the extractive project is generating revenue or turning a profit. By this line of argument, public infrastructure constructed early in the extractives project cycle may provide legitimacy for a democratically elected government, or for a non-democratic one with a perceived need for some form of popular legitimacy. Collier also counts the speed of infrastructure delivery among the main attractive features of RFI contracting. Lin and Wang suggest that RFI may be a suitable model for the construction of what they call "bottleneck-releasing" infrastructure that is associated with RFI host countries' comparative advantage.

Lin and Wang argue that another advantage of RFI is that it addresses the potential for currency mismatch in the down payment of infrastructure loans. Whereas a revenue stream from an infrastructure project would be denominated in domestic currency, the revenues from the extractives component of an RFI deal are generated in global commodity markets. By this line of argument, exchange rate risks related to the down payment of the infrastructure loan may be eliminated if the commodity sales and the infrastructure loan are denominated in the same currency, generally U.S. dollars.

Collier argues that whereas the pledging of resource revenues is useful collateral to unblock obstacles in circumstances where the negotiation and construction phases prove too fraught for standard project finance, governments should not tie up their capital indefinitely. Once the infrastructure—for example, a power station—is built, it becomes low risk, and the government could sell it on to a private operator. According to Collier, "in a capital-scarce, high-risk environment, the governments should not be tying up their limited capital in low-risk, capital-intensive infrastructure that could be operated privately."

Gelb, Lin, Wang, and Wells point to an issue that has been addressed little in the existing literature—namely the level of risk assumed by the banks and companies involved in RFI deals, and the role of concessional finance in mitigating such risk. Once the infrastructure has been completed, which may be well before oil, gas, or mineral production has started, there is an incentive for the government to renege on the contract. Wells argues that a political opposition or a new government is likely to forget that benefits were received early in the extractives project cycle, and might exert pressure to renegotiate. With the investor taking a significant share of operational, economic, and political risk, RFI deals would in that sense be equivalent to nonrecourse loans, and an element of official or semi-official concessional finance to reduce investor risk has so far been a standard component of RFI deals. Gelb suggests that concessional financing arrangements could take the form of interest rate buy-down or partial risk guarantees against the host-country government reneging on the agreement. Lin and Wang argue that, to reduce the pressures for renegotiation, transparency also serves the interest of the banks and companies involved in RFI deals.

Criticism and Risks

The authors of the study, and the commentators, also point to several significant risks inherent in RFI contracting. All of them argue forcefully that the same levels of transparency should apply to all contractual arrangements for resource extraction, including RFI. The main concerns are highlighted in the EITI requirements, as summarized in Clare Short's comment: "in order to address infrastructure and barter provisions efficiently, the EITI requires that stakeholders are able to gain a full understanding or the relevant agreements, contracts, the parties involved, the resources which have been pledged by the state, the value of the benefit stream (for example, infrastructure works), and the materiality of these agreements relative to conventional contracts [...] the comprehensive treatment of such deals is necessary in order to meet EITI requirements."

Other fundamental concerns discussed in the study include a sound fiscal structure to manage revenues generated after the infrastructure investment has been paid down, measures to ensure the quality of the infrastructure and the integrity of the construction process, as well as arrangements for operation and maintenance after the infrastructure has been completed. The importance of efficient measures to address such issues cannot be overstated.

Collier sees the opaque nature of many existing RFI deals as a result of a monopoly situation in the supply of such deals. If there were more providers of RFI deals, "for example, if bilateral donors teamed up with their national resource companies and construction companies," the value of RFI deals could in his view be determined through competition. So far, however, RFI proposals have originated in the form of so-called unsolicited bids, from firms seeking opportunities either on the extractive or the infrastructure side, and then partnering with other firms and a financing institution to build a bankable deal to offer the government (Wells 2013). Unsolicited bids are not uncommon in the construction and the extractive sectors, and several countries have legislation in place to channel unsolicited infrastructure proposals into public competitive processes, thereby encouraging the private sector to propose potentially beneficial project concepts while maintaining the benefits of open tendering. Chile and the Republic of Korea, for example, use a "bonus system," where a 5 to 10 percent bonus is credited to the original proponent's bid in an open bidding round for the tender resulting from the unsolicited project proposal (Hodges and Dellacha 2007).

Wells contends that countries need to evaluate RFI proposals in light of what they might otherwise receive for their resources—and what they would pay to finance associated infrastructure, if financing were to come from other sources. In other words, to address valuation and risk issues, those assessing an RFI option would need to first compare the option's estimated infrastructure costs with the costs of conventional fiscal and investment models—whereby resource revenues would go into the budget, and construction would be financed by the public spending supported by these revenues.

Wells further argues that most of the criticism levied against RFI applies equally to independent contracting of infrastructure and extractive projects, and that there is little evidence to support the conclusion that RFI deals are associated with more corruption than other extractive and construction contracts in the same host countries. In his view, the problem of poor countries' weak ability to negotiate with skilled foreign investors and enforce concluded agreements is a problem to be addressed independent of RFI.

Many of the arguments made in the study, and by the commentators, seek to move beyond positions for or against RFI. As Wells puts it, "RFI models are neither good nor bad for host countries. They should be evaluated like any other business arrangement, and carefully compared to alternative ways of obtaining returns from natural resources or financing infrastructure." Gelb points out that the study "makes useful distinctions between the principles underlying the RFI model and past practices in implementing it, arguing that faults in implementation do not necessarily invalidate the good points of the approach." Clare Short, chair of the EITI, finds that the study "provides useful guidance for how governments can assure good governance and transparency when resource extraction is used to finance infrastructure development. It provides policy makers, contracting parties, and affected communities with a framework for understanding and comparing RFI deals, monitoring their implementation, and assessing both opportunities and risks."

Notes

1. Requirement 4.1 (d) of the EITI Standard stipulates: The multistakeholder group and the Independent Administrator are required to consider whether there are any agreements, or sets of agreements, involving the provision of goods and services (including loans, grants, and infrastructure works), in full or partial exchange for oil, gas, or mining exploration or production concessions or physical delivery of such commodities. To be able to do so, the multistakeholder group and the Independent Administrator need to gain full understanding of the terms of the relevant agreements and contracts, the parties involved, the resources which have been pledged by the state, the value of the balancing benefit stream (for example, infrastructure works), and the materiality of these agreements relative to conventional contracts.

2. A key feature of RFI deals is the commitment of future government revenues for debt servicing of present infrastructure investment. In this sense, the RFI model is closely related to the more common practice of collateralizing debt with future oil receipts. Collateralization of future revenues (CFR) has implications for the sustainability of government debt (the government's ability to service other debt is lowered) and may have legal implications. Many loan agreements, including those of the World Bank under the International Bank for Reconstruction and Development (IBRD) window, include negative pledge clauses that preclude borrowing countries from pledging present or future assets to another creditor. An important legal distinction is the one between arrangements that give rise to claims against the sovereign or a public enterprise ("direct" CFR arrangements), or against a special purpose vehicle (SPV, "indirect" CFR arrangements). Indirect CFR arrangements, in contrast to direct CFR arrangements, are subject to few legal constraints. Often, these transactions are structured in ways that give rise to claims for payment against only the SPV, and not against the government as the originator (see IMF 2003).

3. For an overview of RFI projects in Africa, see Alves (2013) and Foster and others (2009).

PART 2

Resource Financed Infrastructure: Origins and Issues

John J. Beardsworth, Jr., and James A. Schmidt

Disclaimer

This study was drafted by John J. Beardsworth, Jr., and James A. Schmidt of Hunton & Williams LLP. Funding was provided by the World Bank. The findings, interpretations, and conclusions expressed in this publication are entirely those of the authors and should not be attributed in any manner to the World Bank, or its affiliated organizations, or to members of its board of executive directors or the countries they represent.

CHAPTER 1

Introduction

"Angola mode" transactions. "Resources for infrastructure" "deals" or "swaps" or "barter." A new form of financing infrastructure has been created in countries that are wealthy in natural resources—typically hydrocarbons or metal ore—but poor in the infrastructure essential for a growing economy. The form of these transactions involves a package where (i) a government grants a resource development and production license to a private developer, and (ii) the government receives infrastructure pursuant to a financing mechanism linked to the resource activity.

Box 1.1 In a Word

The resource financed infrastructure (RFI) model is a financing model whereby a government pledges its future revenues from a resource development project to repay a loan used to fund construction of infrastructure. The key advantage of the model is that a government can obtain infrastructure earlier than it would have been able to if it had to wait for a resource project to produce revenues. This new financing model resembles aspects of other financing models, and use of the model will raise issues in the same way that every other model does, whether used for a resource development project or an infrastructure construction project.

The transactions have attracted attention because of the novelty of the approach, and drawn criticism because the lack of transparency in the negotiation and implementation of the deals (especially regarding the establishment of a fiscal regime for the resource component and how the infrastructure contracts relate to the financing mechanism) fosters suspicions of corruption and self-dealing among the investors (and their lenders) and the government officials involved. Lack of transparency, and suspicions of corruption and self-dealing, are concerns that, unfortunately, are not limited to these transactions, but arise all too often in many countries in both resource and infrastructure projects. There has also been criticism, as with many projects that use traditional forms of financing, that some of the infrastructure constructed through these deals was of poor quality, involved "vanity" projects that did not meet the country's development needs, and/or was poorly maintained (or not maintained at all) and therefore deteriorated quickly.

These criticisms, even when justified in particular instances, do not necessarily mean that the financing model used in these transactions is flawed. In this study we address three points:

- First, we examine the origins of this new model, which we suggest is most accurately called the "resource financed infrastructure" (RFI) model, to determine whether there was a need for a new financing model at all.
- Second, we unbundle and describe the RFI model and how it works in theory—and can work in practice. We recognize that implementing the model for a specific application in a particular country's circumstances will likely require certain adjustments (as would the implementation of any other model).
- Third, we identify and describe the structural, financial, and operational issues that governments, investors, donors, and other stakeholders might consider when adopting the RFI model for application in a specific transaction.

We have found that the RFI model has its origins in other models used for decades or longer by governments and private companies, and fills gaps between those models. These origins and gaps will become clear as we unbundle and describe the RFI model, and the precursor models from which it developed. In brief, an RFI project starts with the establishment of a fiscal regime for a resource development and production component—as with any resource development project—and continues with the establishment of a credit facility based on the government's pledged revenue stream from the resource component. The government then uses the credit facility for construction of nonassociated infrastructure. The infrastructure component of an RFI transaction can be structured as a government procurement project, with 100 percent government ownership, or in any number of other ways consistent with a public-private partnership (PPP) transaction.

We have found that using the RFI model will raise many of the same issues that exist in the precursor models, and create a few new issues that must be identified and addressed for an RFI transaction to be successful. The RFI model is no better or worse, per se, than any other financing model. If the risks and issues are identified and properly addressed, we believe there are certain circumstances where use of the RFI model can bring substantial benefits to a country and its citizens, primarily by creating a financing mechanism to facilitate construction of infrastructure, and thereby spark economic growth and social benefits, years ahead of what would have been possible under any other model. In the end, the success of a specific RFI transaction depends on proper structuring and implementation.

CHAPTER 2

The Origins of the Resource Financed Infrastructure Model

It is unclear whether the government officials and the teams representing the investors and lenders that negotiated the first transactions that we can now identify as using a variant of the resource financed infrastructure (RFI) model knew they were using a new model, or thought they were just combining existing models in a slightly different way. The negotiation teams involved would doubtless have been aware of existing models, and found themselves addressing a gap between them. By trying to cover this gap in the specific circumstances being negotiated, they ended up creating something that, in hindsight, we can now see as the birth of a new model—the RFI model.

In this chapter we look at the "parents" of the RFI model, the models that were in regular use around the world long before the RFI model was born. We summarize the main features of each model, and then perform a SWOT (strengths, weaknesses, opportunities, threats) analysis of each. At the end of this chapter we identify the gaps between existing models that the RFI model fills. We emphasize that each of these models, when applied to specific transactions, can be significantly modified to address transaction-specific circumstances or the more general market considerations that change over time based on the conditions of the global finance markets.

Traditional Resource Development Model

The traditional resource development model (figure 2.1) has long been used for hydrocarbons, ore/minerals, and other export-oriented projects. For extractive projects, the transaction is based on a licensing regime, typically a petroleum law or a mining law, under which a developer may apply for exploration and eventually development and/or production licenses.

The traditional resource development model starts with a resource development law that sets forth the procedures by which investors may apply for, or sometimes bid for, exploration licenses. In many instances, particularly for non-hydrocarbon resource exploration activities, an investor is allowed to apply

Figure 2.1 Example of a Traditional Resource Development Model

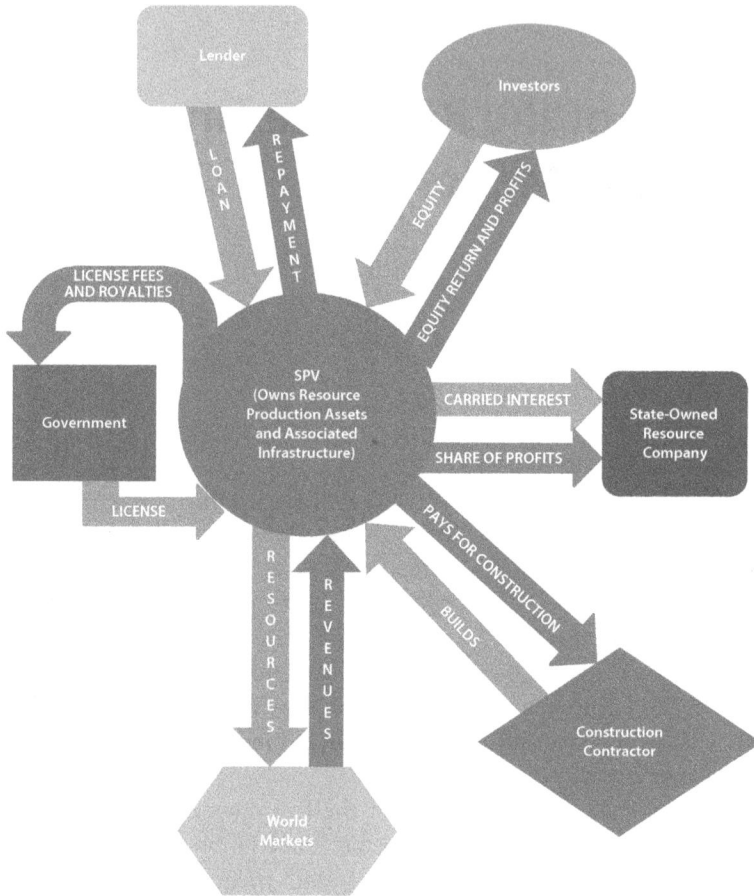

Source: Authors.
Note: SPV = special purpose vehicle.

for an exploration license covering a certain geographic area. The license, when granted, will be of a specified term and remain in effect so long as the investor is diligently undertaking exploration activities. Exploration activities are undertaken with equity investments, and usually have a high risk of failure: Even where initial geologic indicators suggest a probable resource, finding a deposit of sufficient size or quality to be commercially exploited using current technologies is difficult.

Box 2.1 The Investor

In this study we refer to an "investor" or a "developer" as though this entity remained constant throughout the predevelopment, development, and implementation phases of a project. This approach works for understanding the origins of the resource financed infrastructure (RFI) model and the issues to be addressed when contemplating an RFI transaction. In real

box continues next page

Box 2.1 The Investor *(continued)*

projects under most models, however, the investor is not a single, unchanging entity. It may be a consortium of several companies, and the consortium may change membership over time, especially in the case of resource transactions moving from the exploration to the development phase. The investor's identity in project finance and private-public partnership (PPP) model transactions tends to change less frequently before the project achieves financing, particularly when the transaction documents limit the initial investor's ability to reduce its equity holding between the award of a tender through the construction phase, and often for some period of the operations phase of a project. As the identity of the investor changes over time, under any transaction, the talents and resources available to the project will change, as will the issues and negotiation positions of the investor.

Usually the investor must share its exploration findings with the government—in many instances, including core samples from drilling activities. Should the investor abandon its efforts and relinquish the exploration license, other interested parties may review that information and decide whether to undertake new exploration activities in that area—potentially for different resources. Even when a desired resource is located, it can sometimes take several years to undertake additional exploration activities sufficient to determine the likely size of the deposit and the likely costs of developing the resource and bringing it to market. If and when the investor makes the decision to proceed, the investor will apply for a development and production license; if the investor decides not to proceed, the investor will relinquish its rights to the exploration area. *For the purposes of this study, the key conclusion from this discussion is that there is no opportunity to undertake an RFI transaction while the resource investor is in the exploration phase because there is no way to predict revenue streams prior to the development phase.*

In the hydrocarbons sector, particularly for oil and gas exploration, many governments have defined exploration blocks that are auctioned or offered for sale at fixed prices. The exploration licenses for these blocks require a license holder to undertake diligent and continuous exploration activities. After a resource is found, additional time is usually required to prove the extent of the resource with sufficient reliability for the investor to make a decision whether to convert the exploration license into a development and production license.

When an investor becomes confident it has proven the existence of a commercially viable resource, whether hydrocarbon or non-hydrocarbon, the investor will approach the host government and seek to convert its exploration license to a development and production license. The process of converting the exploration license to the development and production license is defined by the relevant resource law, with discretion in certain areas typically reserved for the government to negotiate with each investor. In some cases, the conversion of the exploration license may include allocation of additional exploration areas adjacent to the development and production license area, both to protect the investor from competition and to enable the recovery of investments should the primary development area yield lower amounts of resources than expected. Upon the grant of a development and production license, the investor will bring capital (whether in the form of debt or equity, or more likely a combination of both) to its project for the development and production activities. The funding required is often significant, and the investor seeks a return on investment (including repayment of debt) over time by selling resources in world markets. Investments are typically made in a "ring-fenced" manner, in which funds used to develop a particular resource (say, from an oil production license area) are paid back from revenues from that resource—with profits distributed from revenues in excess of the investment and operating amounts. The typical structure allocates revenues from the resource over the project cycle to ensure first that the development costs are fully recovered, and then that profits are allocated. Thus a government is likely to receive a modest revenue stream in the early years of resource production, and a higher revenue stream later on. In evaluating whether to make an investment, an investor will look to modeled prices of resources over time, the amount and value of "proven" resources in the ground (as established during the exploration phase), and the costs of extracting and processing the resource and delivering the product to world markets.

The government's role in the traditional resource development model is primarily that of a regulator, issuing and enforcing licenses, though certain participation rights may also be reserved for a state-owned resource company. Through these regulatory mechanisms and its other powers, the government will enforce relevant environmental and social laws, and any other laws applicable to the resource development business.

Box 2.2 Dual Role Risks

Where a state-owned resource company becomes part of the "investor," the government will find itself, in essence, on both sides of the negotiations for the issuance and enforcement of resource development and production licenses. In project finance model transactions, the government may take on dual roles to the extent it becomes a lender to the project, a part owner of the project, or the sole offtaker from the project. In a public-private partnership (PPP) model transaction, as discussed below, the government will likely have dual roles.

From the perspective of a transaction model, whether the resource financed infrastructure (RFI) model, the project finance model, or the PPP model, it is a straightforward process to analyze and separate a government's dual, or even multiple, roles. Dual roles can provide another source of revenue to the government if the project is successful, and can also provide the government with insights into the company's operations through participation on the board of directors.

But despite the benefits that can accrue, a government's dual or multiple roles in major transactions have also caused many problems over time, particularly when the government loses the incentive to enforce license and contract rights, or environmental or social standards, because of fear that the state-owned resource company involved will lose its share of profits. These problems are especially acute when the same government ministry is responsible for

box continues next page

Box 2.2 Dual Role Risks *(continued)*

both negotiating and enforcing licenses and project documents, and for supervising the operations of the state-owned resource company.

A full discussion of the risks associated with dual roles in major projects is beyond the scope of this study, but we suggest, at a minimum, that governments ensure at least that the same individuals are not involved in, or responsible for, both sides of the negotiations, or when a potential adversarial situation arises between the government and the project company.

Government revenue from resource projects takes the form of royalties and taxes, and/or production-sharing rights, as prescribed under law and stated in the relevant license. To the extent there is a state-owned company that owns shares in the project or otherwise exercises reserved participation rights, whether as a paid or carried interest, the government may receive additional revenues through dividends. In addition, in resource development projects in some countries the developer has paid "signing bonuses" to the government or the state-owned partner.

In developing a resource extraction project, the developer may make investments outside of the resource location to get products to the market, or to attract workers to its site. These investments may include roads, rail lines, pipelines, port facilities, worker compounds, health clinics, market buildings and houses in worker compounds, and the like. Although they may have some public benefit, these "associated infrastructure" investments are for the primary purpose of facilitating resource extraction. Typically the resource development company pays for, operates, and owns (or retains the right of use) of associated infrastructure for the duration of the resource extraction project.

A SWOT analysis of the traditional resource development model is given in table 2.1.

Table 2.1 Traditional Resource Development Model

Strengths	Weaknesses
• Well-known and well-used model globally.	• Government oversight frequently weak due to financial disparity between the resource developer and regulator.
• Understood by developers, governments, and lenders.	
• Community development frequently required in resource development area.	• Frequently long periods between when development and production licenses are issued and government revenues first received.
• Investment at cost and risk of developers and lenders; products sold to global markets, so government not at risk of overpricing.	• Developers have incentives to build necessary associated infrastructure, but no incentive to otherwise contribute to national development goals.
• Global initiatives, such as the Extractive Industries Transparency Initiative (EITI), seek to enforce transparency.	• Competition frequently not possible, especially for hard minerals. Oil/gas exploration blocks sometimes auctioned.
• Government exposure to costs is limited—investments are undertaken by developers.	• Financing uncertainty can result in long waiting periods for execution.

table continues next page

Table 2.1 Traditional Resource Development Model *(continued)*

Opportunities	Threats
• Investments in associated infrastructure can bring jobs and services to areas outside the licensed resource area.	• Inadequate resource or mining laws can make transactions nontransparent, creating political risks.
• Governments have negotiation leverage at the time when development and production licenses are being negotiated.	• The use of "signing bonuses" can give an appearance of corruption if funds are not clearly applied to national accounts.
	• Civil unrest possible if resource developments (i) appear to create significant wealth for resource developers before any benefits accrue to the population, or (ii) appear not to provide any local (as opposed to national) benefit.

Source: Authors.

Traditional Government Infrastructure Purchasing Model

Governments have long purchased and built infrastructure for their citizens. These projects have been funded with tax revenues, through issuance of bonds, and occasionally through bank borrowing. Developing countries have long used grants and concessional finance (from the World Bank and others) to develop infrastructure. For countries rich in resources under production, revenue from resource royalties and taxes paid to the government, and dividends paid to the state-owned company participating in the resource extraction industry, can fund substantial infrastructure investments.

Under the traditional government infrastructure purchasing model (figure 2.2), there is no private developer, and, where sovereign funds are used, no need to develop a financial model to show lenders or investors that each specific infrastructure investment will produce sufficient revenues to "pay off" the investment. Many of the most basic infrastructure items (such as roads, schools, electricity distribution systems, and hospitals) may not produce any significant revenues directly, but are widely seen as essential items for economic growth—which, in turn, will eventually produce more tax revenues. The government can decide what infrastructure to build, and when to build it—assuming it has, or can borrow the money, to pay for the investments.

Competition can be imposed by a government directly at the construction contract level, because a government tenders directly for engineering, procurement, and construction (EPC) contracts and owner engineer services, among others. On the other hand, a government may ask state-owned design and construction companies (for example, overseen by a roads ministry) to implement the project directly. Even in such a case, there would still likely be competition to supply equipment and raw materials. The effectiveness of the competitive process at any level depends on how well specified the tender documents are, and the transparency of the process used pursuant to applicable procurement

Figure 2.2 Example of a Traditional Government Infrastructure Purchasing Model

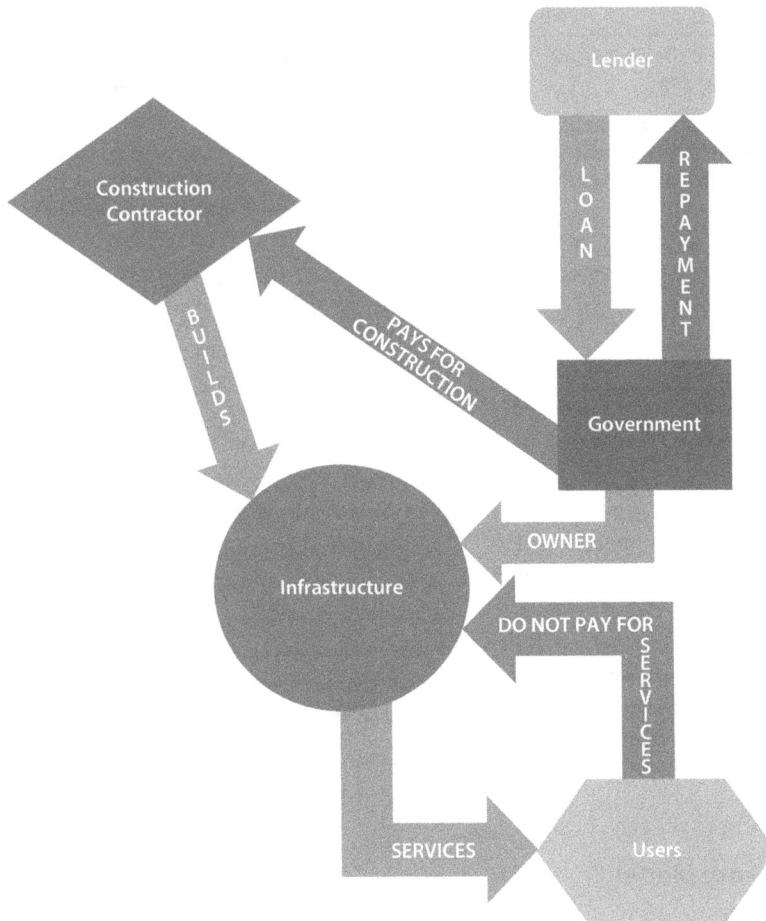

Source: Authors.

laws. Where projects are financed by lenders or grant providers, such funding sources may also impose requirements on tendering processes and/or involve construction supervision consultants, often in the form of tied aid.

The private sector, to the extent it is involved, will serve as a contractor to the government. For example, construction firms may bid to build roads or buildings without taking any ownership interest in the project. In some cases, in both developed and developing countries, corruption has occurred in the form of inflated contract prices accompanied by kickback payments to corrupt officials and politicians. A robust public procurement law with transparent tendering procedures can minimize such events.

A SWOT analysis of the traditional government infrastructure purchasing model is given in table 2.2.

Table 2.2 Traditional Government Infrastructure Purchasing Model

Strengths	Weaknesses
• Government can decide what infrastructure to develop, at what time. • Infrastructure projects can be justified on an economic growth basis, without regard to cash revenues generated from each specific component. • Competition possible for hiring of construction contractors, or for supplying of equipment and materials.	• Ability to build infrastructure depends on having funds available, either from tax revenues or borrowings. • Government borrowing on concessional basis is frequently focused on construction of new infrastructure, rather than maintenance or prudent operation of existing assets. • Certain grant funds are allocated to "vanity" projects, which are frequently not well maintained after construction.
Opportunities	Threats
• Government use of "owner engineer" construction supervisors can improve construction quality. • Robust analysis of costs and benefits of each project can ensure infrastructure is developed in a prudent, and properly phased, order. • A well-organized process for vetting projects and contractors can result in improved transparency and stakeholder inclusiveness, leading to political and community support.	• Risk of corruption as officials administering construction projects can be tempted by bribes. • Inadequate public procurement procedures can lead to nontransparent contracting. • Accepting "tied aid" loans, even on a concessional basis, can lead to inflated charges for infrastructure projects. • Focus on the development of new infrastructure, rather than maintenance of existing assets, can lead to rapid deterioration of infrastructure assets.

Source: Authors.

Project Finance Model

Compared to the models discussed above, the project finance model (figure 2.3) is of more recent origin. Project finance as a model became the key way to bring private capital into infrastructure transactions in developing countries through the late 1980s and remains a vibrant model amid varying credit market conditions, construction contract terms, and the types of projects that governments decide to outsource to the private sector. It is also a key financing model used by the private sector throughout the world for noninfrastructure investments.

Prior to the advent of the project finance model, companies developed projects based on the strength of their balance sheets. Each project undertaken was developed through: (i) sales of shares at the company level, (ii) use of retained earnings from all company activities, and/or (iii) company debt either through the issuance of bonds or taking bank debt on to the company balance sheet. This approach allowed all company assets to be leveraged in support of new businesses or expanded activities, but also meant that any new major activity was a potential "bet the company" risk. The risk that any new activity could drag the entire company into bankruptcy made some boards of directors very cautious, and stifled both expansion and innovation. Under the project finance model, however, a company could protect its overall balance sheet by limiting its

Resource Financed Infrastructure • http://dx.doi.org/10.1596/978-1-4648-0239-3

Figure 2.3 Example of a Project Finance Model

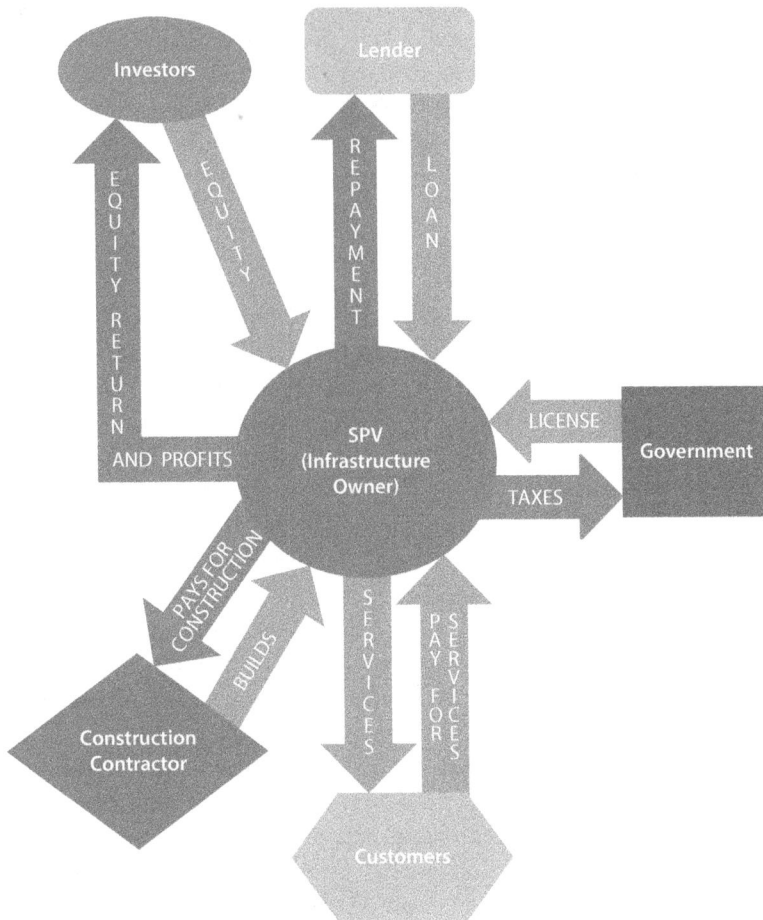

Source: Authors.
Note: SPV = special purpose vehicle.

exposure to the investments made in each project, so failure in one project would not result in a loss of more than the equity committed to that project. This innovation allowed established companies to undertake investments in new activities or at new locations while protecting the rest of the balance sheet.

Over time, the project finance model was also embraced by new, smaller, and dynamic developers who could attract sufficient equity and debt to finance a project. These developers brought technical skills to the matters relevant to a project; financial skills in creating financially viable project documents designed to achieve positive cash flows throughout a project's operating life cycle; and management skills needed to run a business efficiently through the development, construction, and operations phases.

In infrastructure transactions under the project finance model, a developer or a government first identifies and defines an infrastructure project in which the private sector can participate. The interested developer structures the project to shield its balance sheet from unlimited exposure to the project, thereby focusing on the stand-alone sustainability of the project over time. This shielding means that the project must produce, or be predicted to produce, sufficient revenues on a monthly basis to pay for (i) its operations and (ii) a return of and on investment. In other words, the project must be seen as one that can produce revenues sufficient to justify the investment, and regular cash flows to ensure that the project can cover its monthly expenses. Developers, their lenders, and the government all understand that if the project does not bring in enough revenues, or that revenues are not sufficiently level to ensure payment of monthly bills— whether because of poor development work by the developer (or its contractors), nonpayment by offtakers (especially if a government entity is the sole offtaker, as in an independent power project [IPP] selling to a state-owned electricity distribution company), or for any other reason (for example, extended force majeure)—then the project itself will fail. In such a case there would be no recourse, other than as provided in the transaction documents, to the developer, the government, or any other entity. Thus the project is invariably undertaken by a "special purpose vehicle" (SPV), which is a company established, and financed, solely to undertake the project.

The project finance model resembles the development and production phases of the traditional resource development model, but differs significantly from that model. For resource projects the early exploration work, which can require substantial funds, is undertaken on a 100 percent equity basis, and the opportunities for competitively tendering the exploration activities is very limited except, as noted above, for certain oil/gas exploration activities. When a resource developer has an exploration license and makes a find, it normally has the right to convert that exploration license into a development and production license, at which point the project can be considered financeable because of the existence of probable, if not proven, resources. Under the project finance model, however, the amount of early equity investment required before the project can be considered financeable is usually much less than under a resource exploration license, and depends primarily on the identification of a suitable project, the development of appropriate documentation (including licenses), and the creation of a financial model that shows positive cash flows under feasible scenarios.

The government role in a project finance model transaction is, in essence, to grant necessary licenses and then let the project develop and operate. In many cases, the government may also act as the tendering body, directly or through an agency, particularly when a state-owned enterprise will be the sole offtaker of the project (as in the IPP example above). In many cases in developing countries, where the offtaker itself is not creditworthy (and thus that entity's promises to pay under an offtake contract cannot make the SPV creditworthy), a government guarantee may be necessary to make project financing possible. Unlike the resource development model, however, and especially for infrastructure projects, the outputs of the project finance model are often used domestically. Because of affordability concerns, product pricing is of greater concern for the government than under the resource model, where the production is typically sold in global markets.

Resource Financed Infrastructure • http://dx.doi.org/10.1596/978-1-4648-0239-3

For a project finance transaction undertaken by the private sector, the government's revenues are primarily from income taxes on company profits. Where there is a resource component to the project, such as in a mine-mouth coal-fired power plant or a gas-turbine power plant fired on locally sourced natural gas, the government would also receive resource royalties (as in a resource development model transaction, described above). Nevertheless, the primary benefit to the government is that the government gets infrastructure developed—infrastructure that provides services the country's citizens are willing to pay for—without using its own funds. The second main benefit to the government is that the private sector owner will have an incentive to make ongoing payments for operations and maintenance (O&M) over the projected investment life cycle of the project. To keep charges to citizens lower, particularly in the early years of operation when debt service will be high, governments frequently give tax holidays to make the products or services provided by the SPV more affordable, or on-lend concessional financing to lower the prices charged for services.

A SWOT analysis of the project finance model is given in table 2.3.

Table 2.3 Project Finance Model

Strengths	Weaknesses
• Government may obtain infrastructure services without committing material state funds.	• Infrastructure investments require forecasts of regular, timely cash flows to achieve financing.
• Private sector involvement brings expertise in development and operations.	• Does not work when no, or insufficient, revenues are projected from the project, without sovereign supports/subsidies.
• Reliance on project cash flows to repay investments motivates owner to maintain assets over economic life.	• Difficult to structure when cash flows are irregular or "lumpy."
• Model well known to investors, lenders, and other stakeholders.	• Substantial advance work is required to define the project before going out to bid, including defining underlying policy goals.
Opportunities	Threats
• Well-structured projects for sectors where revenue projections support investment are attractive to investors and lenders.	• Poorly structured projects can result in charges that are unaffordable for the population.
• Financial and commercial innovation creates opportunities for more projects.	• Inadequately prepared tender documents can result in low investor interest, or substantial delays between tendering and financing.
• Governments that prepare tendering documents well, and offer appropriate supports, will attract competitive bids.	• Requires strong legal and policy framework to ensure transparent bidding procedures and provide certainty for investors and lenders.

Source: Authors.

Public-Private Partnership Model

The PPP model (figure 2.4) of infrastructure transactions is the newest—or more accurately, the most recently named—infrastructure financing model of the four precursors to the RFI model. The *PPP model* has become a common term for a

Figure 2.4 Example of a Public-Private Partnership Model

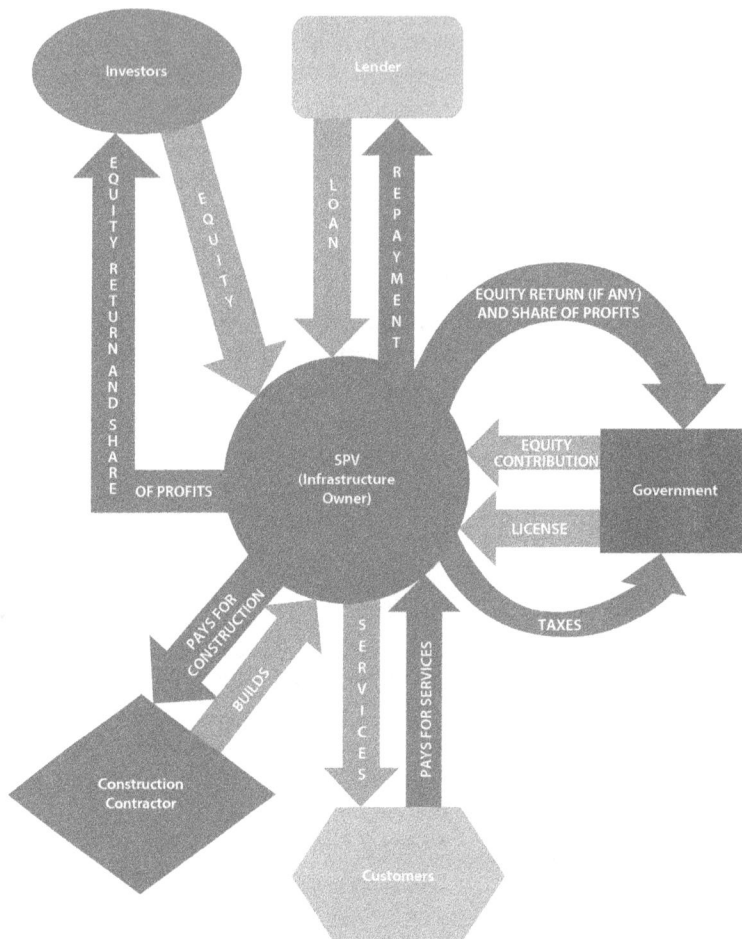

Source: Authors.
Note: SPV = special purpose vehicle.

stand-alone model over the past 10 to 15 years. It resembles the project finance model, and can be considered a variant of it, but the PPP model leaves more room for government involvement both initially and over time. This model is frequently used where a project finance model transaction has been considered, but will not work because of the need to fill a gap in project risks that only the government can fill. Because of the many ways it can be applied, it is a very flexible model.

Under the PPP model, a government makes a decision to invite private sector involvement (both finances and expertise) in a project, and may offer to coinvest in appropriate projects. The PPP model can be viewed as an outgrowth of the French "concession" approach to public services developed many years ago. In this approach, a state agency or municipality that owns a public service entity (such as a water supply system) decides to obtain private sector O&M of that system, together with transferring responsibility for ongoing investments for a period of many years. The resulting "concession" is a PPP for the provision of those services. In other situations, a government may offer to transfer land or other existing assets, together with "free" licenses, in exchange for a shareholding in the project SPV. As with the project finance model, the PPP model can be effected through a competitive tender. Depending on the structuring of the transaction components, the revenues need not pay for the full investment, so long as the revenues cover the O&M expenses of the project, debt service for loans that are in the SPV's name, and returns of and on the developer's equity investment.

Developers have been attracted to the full range of PPP model projects in many countries. In some instances a PPP project can be little more than a management contract for a single business. At the other end of the scale a PPP project can be almost identical to one under a project finance model, as many project financed projects need government participation, such as the use of an existing industrial facility or site, in exchange for a minority equity shareholding. In the end, both the private developer and the government can declare that they are "partners" in providing infrastructure services in a PPP model infrastructure transaction. This flexibility makes the model robust and useful.

A SWOT analysis of the PPP model of infrastructure transactions is given in table 2.4.

Table 2.4 Public-Private Partnership Model

Strengths	Weaknesses
• Very flexible model allows substantial room to structure specific transactions to meet government and other stakeholder needs.	• Flexibility means that each transaction must be carefully developed on a custom basis—multiple models for PPP must be carefully analyzed.
• Government involvement can reduce private investor's perceived risk.	• Where transaction is not financed based on revenue flows from the specific project, ongoing government support for the project will be required.
• Appropriate sharing of risks can limit government exposure to private investor's poor performance, and private investor's exposure to economic or market risks outside its control.	• Underperforming projects may require substantial public support unless the government is willing to let the project fail.
Opportunities	Threats
• Flexibility of model allows governments to attract private sector expertise and management skills in areas previously off-limits to the private sector.	• Poor preparation and/or execution of projects can result in excessive profits for the private sector partner and/or inadequate performance of contract services.
• Transparent tendering process and careful preparation of projects will result in optimum results for governments.	• Government partnership in project does not relieve government of obligation to monitor project and perform regulatory oversight.
• Mobilizing private sector experience to support identified public policy goals improves sustainability.	• Underperforming projects can result in bankruptcy of the project company unless equity investors, lenders, or the government provide additional funding.

Source: Authors.

Mind the Gaps

We have now looked at four models that were in use at the time the RFI model was born. Clearly these models were useful for many projects, but just as clearly these models left gaps that remained to be filled. What were these gaps?

- The traditional resource development model is an excellent way for governments to monetize their natural resources, and obtain funds for providing public infrastructure. *But* the time between "first shovel" in the extraction activity and the beginning of the government's "revenue stream" that could be used to obtain infrastructure often approached 10 years. The gap to be filled was to find a way for a government to obtain infrastructure without waiting for the revenue stream.
- The traditional government infrastructure purchasing model provides a clear way for a government to identify and obtain infrastructure—but only as much as funds allow. The government may need to justify the investment to donors and other potential lenders based on an economic growth model or on other general health and welfare parameters, but there is no need to prove revenues directly from the particular investment itself. *But* in developing countries the ability to obtain funds, even through sovereign borrowing, was limited, and many developing countries—though rich in natural resources—had exhausted their ability to raise funds using this model. Worse, in many cases donors were willing to fund construction of infrastructure (and even encouraged governments to use available funds for this purpose), but little attention or effort was made to ensure sustainability. Thus with poor O&M, many expensive infrastructure projects crumbled, leaving governments with both unusable infrastructure and high sovereign debts. The gap to be filled was to find a way to allow a government to obtain infrastructure for essential services, even when it could not raise or borrow funds on a sovereign basis.
- The project finance model is an excellent way for a government to attract investments in infrastructure on a nonrecourse basis to the government, as the private sector takes on the risks of completion and operation, but only when the cash flow is sufficient to cover a project's operating and capital costs on a timely basis. This model is therefore very useful for funding, for example, telecommunications, electricity, tourism, and airport investments, where middle-class and business customers can be relied on to pay for services, and the private sector is able to manage the completion and operational risks. *But* in developing countries there are many essential services that are needed by the population, including clean water, primary schools, and better roads. Governments know that providing these essential services will spark economic growth that will increase incomes and thereby tax revenues, but also know that until growth starts many people cannot pay for these essential services. The gap to be filled was to find a way to allow a government to obtain infrastructure with the involvement of the private sector, on a nonrecourse basis, when there is no expectation that the revenues from the project will pay for that investment.

- The PPP model provides a clear and flexible way for a government to attract investments in infrastructure. The risks of completion and operation are taken on by the private sector for those projects with a clear cash flow (whether from project revenues, another committed source of revenues, through a government commitment to pay, or through a combination of sources), sufficient to cover the developer's operating and capital costs. The flexibility of the model inspired a wide variety of creative approaches, and made the model more useful for projects with marginal revenues, or where the government could contribute existing assets to lower the capital costs of the project and thus the charges to users. *But* as flexible as this model is, projects using it could not avoid the ultimate truism that investments must ultimately be paid for, and that a secure and predictable cash flow from some specific source, even if a sovereign payment commitment of revenue shortfalls, is necessary to achieve financing of infrastructure. The gap to be filled was to find a way to identify a cash flow that would allow the financing of infrastructure on a nonrecourse basis to the government, while also enabling the type of flexibility inherent in the PPP model to obtain the benefits of private sector participation in providing essential government services.

The development of the RFI model was driven by the need to fill these gaps in projects where a government was eager to obtain additional infrastructure for its citizens, a resource developer was eager to obtain access to valuable natural resources, and a lender was willing to make loans to connect and facilitate achievement of these two desires.

Resource Financed Infrastructure • http://dx.doi.org/10.1596/978-1-4648-0239-3

CHAPTER 3

Resource. Financed. Infrastructure.

The resource financed infrastructure (RFI) model (figure 3.1) is a mechanism through which a government can obtain essential infrastructure without it having to produce sufficient revenues to support its financing. It will work when a government wants to involve the private sector in the project, and also wants the project to be built with limited or nonrecourse financing to protect the national treasury from credit exposure. It will work when a government does not have funds available to invest currently, and cannot borrow on a sovereign basis perhaps due to covenants with the International Monetary Fund (IMF) or other donor agencies. It will work when a government has a resource that it licenses for development and production to a private developer, and as part of that licensing process, or potentially in tandem with or following the grant of the license, the government can borrow against its expected revenue stream from the resource development project.

In essence, the RFI model involves an interlinked three-step process:

- Agree on a resource development and production license with a resource developer seeking to convert its exploration license to a development and production license. When issued, the development and production license must have a firm development timeline and a fiscal regime that provides clear revenue flows to the government when the resource is under production. These revenue flows may include production-sharing credits or royalties, other tax receipts, and the dividends payable to any government-owned entity with an ownership interest in the project.
- Pledge the government's interest in some or all of the revenue flows it will receive from the resource production project to a lender in exchange for a credit facility to be paid back (both principal and accrued interest) solely from the pledged revenue stream. For example, the government may pledge just the production royalties, or it may pledge all revenues. In some cases, particularly in hydrocarbon production-sharing agreements, the assets pledged may include the government's rights (directly or through a national oil company) to revenues from the sale of its share of "cost oil or gas" and

Figure 3.1 Example of a Resource Financed Infrastructure Model with Government Ownership of the Infrastructure Component

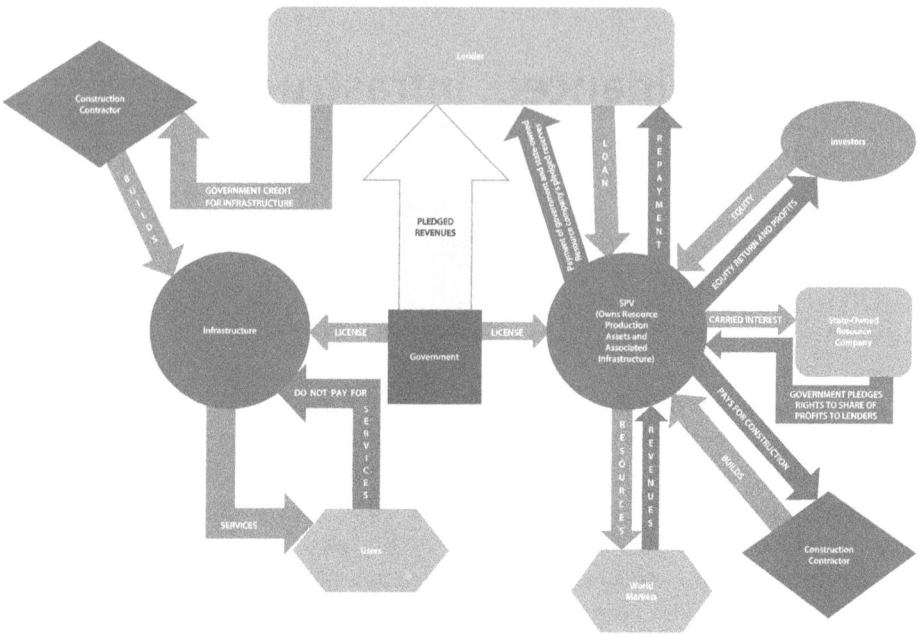

Source: Authors.
Note: SPV = special purpose vehicle.

"profit oil or gas." The greater the revenue flow pledged, the larger the potential credit facility that the government can obtain.

- Access the government's credit facility to obtain infrastructure by contracting with entities that specialize in the development and construction of the specific types of infrastructure to be built. The credit facility would provide the funds for the construction and, potentially, the operations and maintenance (O&M) of the infrastructure, and repayment of the debt would be from the pledged revenue streams from the resource production project. Once the debt is repaid, or annual revenues exceed the amount that needs to be repaid in any year, the balance of the resource revenue stream would be paid to the government.

Box 3.1 Three Government Counterparties for One Project?

As described above, a government using the resource financed infrastructure (RFI) model would agree separately with a resource developer (for the development and production license), a lender (for the credit facility), and the infrastructure developer (for the infrastructure component). It is important that stakeholders address these components separately, and the

---

box continues next page

Box 3.1 Three Government Counterparties for One Project? *(continued)*

differing interests and risks that each party has in the structuring, negotiation, and implementation phases. Considering an RFI transaction as an interrelated set of three interactions clearly puts the government in the middle, and in control, of the process.

Experience to date, however, shows that as governments have started negotiating RFI transactions, the three counterparties frequently have already formed alliances and coordinated their positions. Sometimes the resource developer assumes responsibility for coordinating construction of the infrastructure. Sometimes the lender will offer concessional finance so long as particular contractors are used—contractors that may not be optimally qualified for the types of infrastructure the government requires. Sometimes the negotiations start at an intergovernmental level, where an offer is made for foreign direct investment (FDI) in both resource production and infrastructure construction, on a "package deal" basis, with financing from a state development bank as part of the deal.

It is not surprising that a government would seek to promote the interests of its resource and construction companies in foreign markets, and might use state development assistance to further these commercial interests. The host government, meanwhile, must also ensure that it protects its national interests. Sometimes the consortium the investors offer as part of a package deal may make the most sense for a transaction. Sometimes the resource developer may also be best suited to undertake the infrastructure construction. But not always. By considering and negotiating the three components of the RFI transaction separately, and determining whether a proposed consortium participant is ideal for each component, a government's likelihood of achieving success in an RFI transaction is greatly enhanced.

The Resource Financed Infrastructure Model: Similar to Its Parents, But a Unique Child

The RFI model is based on the traditional resource development model in that it starts with the identification of a licensee to develop a resource development project. It differs from that model in that it may, as discussed below, require finding a resource development licensee who can bring a lender to the project. This lender must be willing to provide the infrastructure development credit to the government on a nonrecourse (or at least limited recourse) basis against a pledge of the government's future expected revenue stream from the resource development project (figure 3.2).

The RFI model is based on the project finance model in that it involves building new infrastructure with nonrecourse financing based on projected (and pledged) revenue flows. It differs from that model in that the pledged revenue streams are not the revenues to be derived from the infrastructure investment itself, but from the government's future revenue streams from the resource development component.

The RFI model is also based on the traditional government infrastructure purchasing model in that the government can decide what infrastructure it wants to build with the credit facility, just as the government can—within the limits

Figure 3.2 Example of a Resource Financed Infrastructure Model with a PPP Coinvestor in the Infrastructure Component

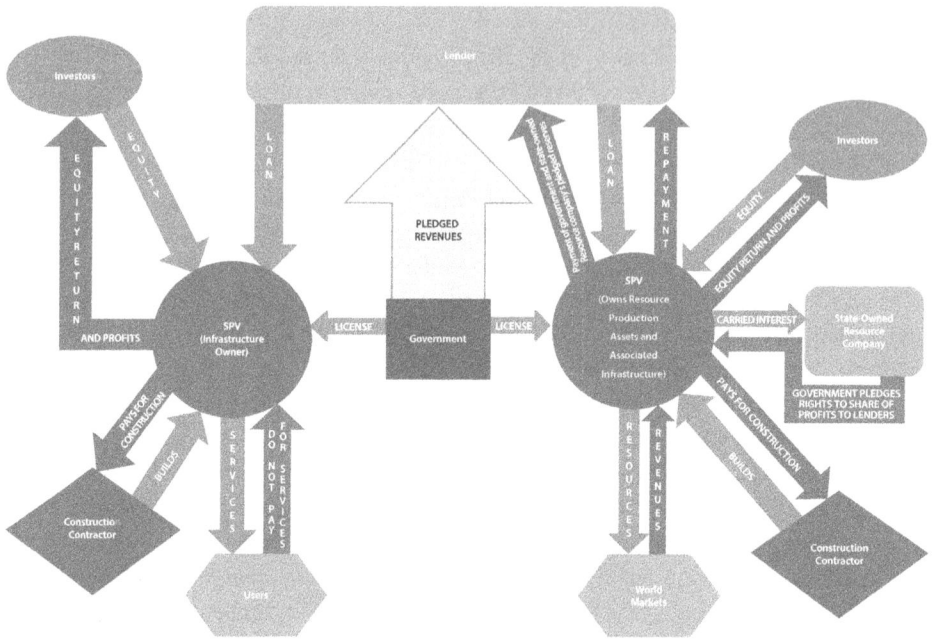

Source: Authors.
Note: SPV = special purpose vehicle; PPP = public-private partnership.

included in any loan documents—decide what infrastructure to build with a sovereign loan facility. The RFI model differs from that model in that a government finances the infrastructure not with sovereign debt, but with a nonrecourse loan against its future revenue streams from the resource development component. If the resource development component fails or produces revenues below expectations, the government would not be liable for any revenue shortfall—as it would be under a sovereign loan agreement.

And finally, the RFI model is based on the very flexible PPP model in that the infrastructure construction process may involve the private sector in a number of ways. The RFI model differs from the PPP model in that an RFI transaction involves resource development, a pledge of the government's resource project revenues, and the construction of infrastructure—but the construction of the infrastructure need not involve the private sector as an equity investor or partner. As discussed below, we believe incorporating characteristics of the PPP model in the infrastructure construction components of an RFI transaction would likely yield substantial benefits to a government.

In the following chapters we discuss a number of financial, structural, and operational issues that the RFI model presents, and that it is commendable to consider before deciding to use an RFI model approach in a specific transaction. As an overview of our discussion of these issues, table 3.1 presents a summary SWOT analysis of the RFI model.

Table 3.1 Resource Financed Infrastructure Model

Strengths	Weaknesses
• The model provides a new financing opportunity for resource-rich governments of countries that need basic infrastructure. • The resource component is based on the well-known resource development model. • Governments can pledge future resource revenue streams to obtain credit facility to develop infrastructure. • Infrastructure components may be developed either as direct government procurement or through PPP types of structures. • Government may obtain non- or limited-recourse financing for infrastructure construction, based on forecast and pledged revenues from the resource component.	• The new model is not yet well known or used by most lenders and investors; therefore, there are few (if any) examples of its successful implementation. • Using debt to build infrastructure with repayment linked to revenue streams from a resource development project will likely create higher capitalized interest than under other models. • The RFI model cannot be used during the period of resource exploration licenses because the revenue stream from resource production activities must be certain enough to support repayment of the government credit facility.
Opportunities	Threats
• Where the government cannot use the project finance model, and cannot obtain sovereign credits to develop infrastructure, an RFI model transaction provides a new opportunity for development and economic growth. • The RFI model is most appropriate for projects that stimulate economic growth, or create social benefits, that exceed the borrowing cost of the government credit. • Government revenues from the resource component, in excess of the funds necessary to pay off the credit facility, remain the property of the government, and would be paid to the government.	• Governments must take responsibility for ensuring that infrastructure components are well designed, well supervised, and well implemented. • Because the lender will look to pledged resource revenue streams for repayment, it is not likely to devote the same attention to the infrastructure components as in a project finance transaction. • Ongoing sustainability of infrastructure must be considered before construction begins, or infrastructure may deteriorate quickly. • Contracting limitations for infrastructure acquisition in the terms of the government credit facility may encourage use of less-qualified contractors, or result in unreasonably high costs of construction.

Source: Authors.
Note: PPP = public-private partnership.

CHAPTER 4

Early Experience with Resource Financed Infrastructure Transactions

To date there have been relatively few resource financed infrastructure (RFI)-type transactions completed, and public information is available for only a few of them. Outside observers of those transactions, from nongovernmental organizations (NGOs) to national parliaments, have raised questions as to the fairness and value of the transactions, as well as suspicions of bad faith dealing (or worse) on both sides of the transactions. Of course, any transaction under any model can be poorly or corruptly executed; there is no particular element of the RFI model that creates higher levels of these risks. But the newness of the RFI model, and a general lack of understanding of it, has created heightened levels of suspicion, which, combined with lack of transparency, has resulted in publicly voiced doubts.

Moreover, the parties (governments, developers, and lenders) who undertook the earliest transactions that can now be seen as the first under the RFI model may not have understood the implications of their new approach. Only in hindsight can the transactions be termed faulty, particularly the infrastructure construction components, even if the overall structure of the RFI transaction as executed was essentially sound.

The limited public information on early RFI-type transactions, particularly regarding infrastructure construction components, may frustrate outside observers keen on improving the transparency of government contracting. It can also be considered a reasonable outgrowth of the concerns over confidentiality that arise under any model, especially on the pricing of the infrastructure. As in the resource development sector, a coordinated effort to make infrastructure contracting by governments more transparent would be a useful exercise, so long as the additional transparency does not stifle price competition for new projects.

In the following chapters, we consider a number of specific issues gleaned from the available documentation on RFI-type transactions to date. We believe there are some key issues for all stakeholders to consider before using the RFI model for a specific transaction. This list is not exhaustive, and does not include the much longer list of issues that will arise in negotiating and finalizing specific

RFI transactions. The next three chapters focus on the categories of financial, structural, and operational issues.

Box 4.1 A Model Timeline?

The resource financed infrastructure (RFI) model may be appropriate for a transaction where (i) a government cannot obtain sufficient resources, on a sovereign basis, to build necessary infrastructure; (ii) the necessary infrastructure will not produce sufficient revenues to finance on a project finance basis; and (iii) the government has a natural resource for which a development and production license is under negotiation, and which could be linked to a credit facility and infrastructure components. This conclusion does not mean, however, that the RFI model can be used only after all sovereign credit sources are exhausted, or only until project finance or public-private partnership (PPP) transactions can attract investor interest on a stand-alone basis.

Even where a government is contemplating an RFI transaction, there may be sectors (such as telecommunications or electricity generation) for which the project finance or PPP model can be used. A government will also be deriving revenue on an ongoing basis from taxes, asset sales, and other sources, and parts of those funds can be used for construction of infrastructure.

In other words, there is no "timeline" or set of milestones that all countries must consider when moving between one financing model and another. It is likely, because of the cost of RFI projects (as discussed below), that the RFI model is best used only when a new resource project is projected to materially increase a government's revenue streams in a few years. Because the size of the projected revenue stream from each new revenue project must grow at least as fast as the country's economy to be considered "material," the RFI model is likely to be used more in small, undeveloped economies and less as an economy grows—at which point project finance and PPP projects, and direct government purchasing, will become more common. But even in a fairly developed economy, a very large resource discovery may make an RFI transaction an attractive option.

CHAPTER 5

Financial Issues

Unbundling the Main Financing Characteristics

As discussed above, the main financing characteristics of a resource financed infrastructure (RFI) transaction are threefold. First, an RFI transaction requires a resource development component that is forecast to provide a revenue stream to the government as the resources begin to reach the market and resource activity reaches profitability. As with any resource development project, there is significant uncertainty and risk in assessing the government's future revenue stream from the resource component. First, early assessments of the resource during the exploration phase may prove to be inaccurate as development begins, or early assessments of the cost of development and production may prove to be understated. Whether for these reasons or because global prices for the resource go down, the investor may abandon the resource development project, resulting in no revenues. Or, less drastically:

- The government's revenue stream may start significantly later than initially forecast if the resource development timing slips.
- The amount of the revenue stream may be substantially lower than forecast if, for example:
  - The amount of resource produced is lower than that forecast, either in any one year or overall.
  - The cost of extraction is higher than forecast.
  - The sale price of the resource is lower than forecast.

These revenue risks affect both the resource developer and the government, but affect the resource developer (and its lender) much more than the government. The developer must commit substantial funds to start the resource development phase, including for the construction of associated infrastructure. Revenues are realized only when the first resources are produced and reach the market. The government's risk (of receiving revenues lower and later than forecast at the time the resource production license is granted) is that it has selected and licensed the "wrong" developer, and that another developer could have developed the resource faster and cheaper, and achieved higher prices.

Second, an RFI transaction requires valuing the forecast revenue stream from the resource production component, and deciding how much of that forecast revenue stream to borrow and invest in infrastructure today. This calculation may be as simple as determining how much a lender would agree to lend against the forecast revenue stream on a nonrecourse basis. Experience to date shows that a lender using the resource development financial model (that is, a lender that has decided to lend to the resource developer to develop the resource extraction component) is in the best position to agree to lend more against a pledge of the government's forecast revenue stream from that same resource extraction project.

Just as the resource developer has a limit on how much money it can borrow for developing the resource component (the rest being injected as equity contributions), there will be a limit on how much of the forecast revenue stream a lender will be willing to lend to a government. The calculation of the government borrowing limit will be related to a number of factors, in particular the sensitivity analysis done on the certainty of the government revenue stream in amount and over time, and the strength of the nonrecourse provisions in the credit agreement should the pledged revenue stream prove inadequate to pay off the outstanding loan during the period the government revenues are pledged.

Box 5.1 Revenue Anticipation Financing

A variation on the resource financed infrastructure (RFI) model would be used in a situation where a resource development project has been licensed, is completing the development process, and is just starting production. As the government revenue stream starts to flow as royalties are paid, this new source of revenue could be pledged against a new loan. The result, which we would call a "revenue anticipation financing" (RAF) model, can also be used whenever a government has a specific source of revenue that is not otherwise committed for servicing existing debt, and is not needed for ongoing government expenses. The RAF model would look much like the RFI model, except that the government would not have the benefit of obtaining the infrastructure years in advance of the resource revenue stream starting. On the other hand, the risk of the revenue stream not materializing would be much lower, and the predictability of the revenue stream will be much higher, once production is under way. And because the funds would be available to pay for the infrastructure loan upon completion of each infrastructure asset, the cost of the infrastructure (including interest accrued before loan repayments begin) would also be lower.

The RAF model would involve further analysis of the resource production project and updating the financial model of the government revenue stream, agreeing on a credit facility against the pledge of that revenue stream (as in the RFI model), and then contracting for infrastructure whether through government purchasing or through a public-private partnership (PPP) (as in the RFI model).

Third, an RFI transaction involves using the credit facility resulting from the pledge of the forecast revenue stream from the resource component. There are two important aspects of this component. The first is deciding what infrastructure to invest in, and the second is contracting for that work. In theory, a government would follow its normal procurement procedures to conduct an open international tender to get the best quality and price on the infrastructure, using the credit from the pledge of the forecast revenue stream on the resource component to pay for the infrastructure. In practice, because most transactions to date have involved concessional financing, a "cost" of the concessional financing is that use of the credit must be according to the lender's procurement rules, which may limit the sources from which goods or services may be purchased with proceeds from the credit. This reality is not unique to RFI transactions, but applies in many cases where concessional finance is made available to a government.

Using the credit facility from a pledge of a forecast revenue stream in an RFI transaction to purchase infrastructure raises the issue of determining how much of the credit facility to consider impaired or drawn for each project. This is a unique and, we believe, poorly understood issue that affects RFI projects. Two examples will highlight the issue.

Consider a project finance infrastructure transaction that requires a $100 million loan, which carries a 5 percent interest rate, and which is drawn down in equal monthly installments over a 24-month construction period. Simple interest accrues during the construction period, and at the end of the 24-month period $5 million of the accrued interest is added to the initial loan amount, for a total debt liability at commissioning of $105 million. At the end of construction, revenues start and no further interest accrues that adds to the outstanding loan amount.

Now consider an RFI transaction where the same infrastructure is built, and that requires the same $100 million loan drawn down over the same 24-month construction period. But assume that the loan agreement provides that interest accrues not just for the two years of construction of the infrastructure (which would be the same $5 million as of the commissioning date of the infrastructure), but that interest continues to accrue for a six-year period (that is, for four years past the commissioning of the infrastructure component) during which the resource component of the RFI transaction is under development. Assume the resource component is completed on time, and the forecast government resource stream is immediately sufficient to service the infrastructure loan, so no further interest is added to the loan principal after the sixth year. The loan principal at the time the resource project starts producing revenues for the government would not be just the $105 million from the moment the infrastructure was completed, but would be $125 million—reflecting four more years of capitalized interest at 5 percent on $100 million, assuming simple interest. Both these examples ignore any effect of periodic capitalization of accrued interest, which would only make the gap between the project finance and RFI loan balances at the start of repayment even greater.

As these examples show, what would have been a $105 million debt in a project finance transaction, where debt servicing starts immediately upon completion of the infrastructure component, becomes a $125 million debt in an RFI transaction because the repayment starts four years later, when the resource component starts producing the revenue stream the government pledged for repayment of the loan. Both debts are based on the same engineering, procurement, and construction (EPC) costs of $100 million—the difference is the accrued interest.

The above discussion illustrates that where infrastructure can be built on a project finance basis, doing so is less expensive than using an RFI credit facility for a construction project of the same amount. On the other hand, because the project finance model can be used only where revenues from the project are sufficient to pay for the costs of the project, an RFI credit may be the least-cost option for obtaining essential infrastructure that cannot generate sufficient revenue to support a project finance transaction.

Box 5.2 Pay the Interest?

Some critics have suggested that the cost of infrastructure in a resource financed infrastructure (RFI) transaction can be "reduced" if the government simply pays the interest following the completion of the infrastructure components, until the pledged resource revenue stream starts. In such a situation, the loan, including capitalized interest, would be the same as the loan amount in a project finance transaction. This suggestion has some appeal, because it is true that infrastructure purchased with a credit facility in an RFI transaction will be associated with the significant additional cost of capitalized interest.

But there are two problems with the suggestion. First, even if the government has sufficient funds to pay interest on the infrastructure loan, it probably has better uses for those funds (such as buying additional infrastructure or paying for maintenance on existing infrastructure) than to pay interest on a loan that would otherwise not be required. Second, although the interest is accruing and will be capitalized with the infrastructure loan, the loan is a nonrecourse loan payable only from the pledged revenue stream. It is also a loan that likely has a concessional interest rate. So although the interest on the infrastructure loan will accrue for the period between the completion of the infrastructure and the beginning of the resource revenue stream, it is unclear why a government would pay out of its own resources against a low-interest, nonrecourse loan.

Valuation of Resource Financed Infrastructure Exchanges

There has been much concern among observers and critics of RFI transactions that governments are "giving away too much" for the infrastructure they "receive" in these projects, or that the price of the infrastructure received is "inflated" and does not reflect "good value." These criticisms seem to arise most often among those who characterize an RFI transaction as a simple "barter" or "swap," rather than as a multicomponent transaction under a new financing model.

Many projects under other models are also criticized as providing poor value, or yielding inadequate compensation for resources. Government procurement projects, particularly when not going well, are regularly reported as being the result of corruption. Project finance transactions, even when well structured and competitively tendered, are the subject of complaints regarding the prices charged, and the profits made, by the owners. Resource projects, in particular, are the subject of intense scrutiny because of their size and the scope of their revenues and profits—although attention is seldom paid to the cost of the development, including the sometimes massive amounts invested for associated infrastructure.

We do not, in short, see these criticisms as unique to the RFI model. Rather, the criticisms reflect global challenges that depend on several variables: What were the circumstances under which the original resource exploration license was issued? Was it granted pursuant to relevant law? Was the resource development and production license properly negotiated and granted, consistent with law, and with the most favorable royalty and tax regime possible? Will the resources be sold at appropriate prices, or will the resource prices realized by the resource operator be inappropriately depressed (for example, by making "sweetheart" deals with an offshore affiliate, which can then resell the resource for the full market price)? These questions are as valid for an RFI transaction as for any other resource development project.

Are the terms of the credit agreement the best available under the circumstances, with the fewest restrictions on the sources of goods and services that can be purchased with the proceeds? Does the amount of capitalized interest in the infrastructure credit reflect a reasonable estimate of how long it will take for the government to be entitled to revenues from the resource component? Such questions are valid both for RFI transactions and for any government procurement project using sovereign credit, as well as for any project finance or PPP project that allows a "pass-through" or "true-up" of financing terms.

And was the pricing of each infrastructure component established in a transparent and competitive manner? This question applies to every transaction under every model. In an RFI context, structuring and addressing the overall transaction with a focus on isolating and optimizing each component will answer the question of whether all parties achieved a good result.

Properly structuring and optimizing each component of an RFI deal will not automatically address all concerns about value in a transaction. There are any number of ways—for technical, commercial, or other reasons—that an RFI transaction could deliver poor value to a government, even when structured well from the economic and legal perspectives. It is important that each stakeholder take appropriate steps to protect its interests at every stage of negotiation and implementation of an RFI transaction, as in any transaction under any other model.

Box 5.3 The Project Implementation Unit

Critics label some governments as incapable of negotiating complex projects. According to their logic, a highly complex resource financed infrastructure (RFI) transaction leaves a government unable to counter the terms offered by a consortia of a development bank flanked by infrastructure and resource developers; perhaps supported by a foreign government; and accompanied by a small army of engineers, financiers, lawyers, and other consultants. Moreover, the critics assert that the scales are inherently against the government because the investor group's business is to negotiate these projects, and for many government officials (unless there is an active hydrocarbon exploration and production industry), the RFI transaction they will negotiate will be the first and perhaps only one of their careers.

A government acts through the people that work for it, and the answer to the criticism that a government does not have adequately experienced experts to negotiate an RFI transaction is: the government can get more and better experts. The World Bank and other donors have long used the instrument of the project implementation unit (PIU) to assist a government in improving its capacity to undertake complex projects. A PIU is set up within the government ministry that will have lead responsibility for the project and is funded by a dedicated revenue source, frequently provided by the donor agency itself. The PIU is then staffed with local and international experts, under long- or short-term contracts as appropriate for the specific project.

Structuring, negotiating, implementing, and supervising an RFI transaction is the type of large, complex, very-high-value project that justifies the creation and adequate staffing of a dedicated PIU.

Relationship to the Fiscal Regime

As with the question of value discussed above, most criticisms of RFI fiscal regimes are among observers who characterize an RFI transaction as a swap or barter, rather than as a transaction under a new financing mechanism. Such observers state that there should be some equivalence between the amount or value of the resource in the ground (and to which the resource developer is being given access) and the amount or value of the infrastructure the country will receive under the first phase of an RFI transaction. It may be that in early RFI transactions the components were poorly structured, and the link between resource development and infrastructure construction was not transparent.

Box 5.4 Is Confidentiality Habit Forming?

We agree that an overall lack of transparency makes it difficult for outside observers to judge whether a government has gotten a "good deal" in a resource financed infrastructure (RFI) transaction. But lack of transparency is not unique to RFI transactions. Many investors, their

box continues next page

Box 5.4 Is Confidentiality Habit Forming? *(continued)*

contractors, and even their lenders require strict confidentiality around the negotiation process and the terms of signed documents. This fact applies to almost every contract under every model, though some progress has been made regarding payments related to resource projects through the Extractive Industries Transparency Initiative (EITI).

There are some legitimate commercial reasons to protect negotiation positions before documents are signed, and certainly good reason to protect intellectual property and trade secrets. But it may be that much of the insistence on confidentiality is simply habit, driven by the fact that everyone at the signing table knows what the documents say, and only those outside the room will complain about a lack of transparency. Where companies are involved, the interested outsiders would be the owners of the companies, but where a government is involved, it is all the citizens of the country that have an interest in what their public servants have done.

Although outside the scope of this study, it may be time to consider, or reconsider, whether the pervasive promises of confidentiality routinely and mutually demanded and agreed upon are in the best interests of a country's citizens, or even the interests of a given project.

The fiscal regime of a resource development and production project, whether under the traditional resource development model or the RFI model, is the methodology by which revenues from the sale of the commodity are allocated to the parties after the costs of extraction, necessary processing, marketing, and delivery are paid. Part of the remaining funds will be allocated to the resource developer as fees and dividends, and part will be allocated to the government and/or the state-owned resource development partner in the project as royalties, taxes, and dividends. The fiscal regime may include the allocation of "cost" and "profit" components, and may also include distribution of part of the commodity produced in kind. In a traditional resource development model transaction, establishing the fiscal regime, and the other provisions of the development and production license, is the end of the transaction-structuring process from the government's point of view.

For an RFI transaction, by contrast, establishing the fiscal regime of the resource component is the government's first step in the transaction-structuring process. The resource component fiscal regime forms the basis on which the government revenues are forecast, then pledged to obtain the credit for construction of the infrastructure component. The government and the resource investor may not even negotiate the fiscal terms of the resource production license if a fiscal regime is already established by law or through a bidding process, in which case that fiscal regime is applied and supplemented with whatever additional agreements are necessary.

The government then pledges its forecast revenue stream, and agrees to the terms of a credit facility with a maximum amount that is somewhat less than the full pledged amount. As in other financing models, there is a "loan-to-value" limit on a pledged asset. In a project finance transaction, for example, the developers will try to "leverage" their equity investments with as much debt as possible, but the lenders will push back on the amount of debt in the project to ensure the loan is secure even if the project revenues do not consistently achieve the forecast levels. For an RFI transaction, the limit of the government credit facility will be tied to the government's forecast revenue streams from the resource component. The value of the government revenue streams from the resource component that are not pledged to service the credit facility remain government owned, whether they are revenues in excess of the debt service amount in a year while the credit facility is outstanding, or the revenues from the resource project after the credit facility is repaid.

The credit facility is then drawn down to purchase infrastructure; as discussed above, the infrastructure purchased may be of a kind that cannot be separately project financed. We recommend that the infrastructure purchased be of a kind that will likely cause economic growth or social welfare benefits valued at a higher rate than the interest rate on the credit facility. In other words, where the cost in lost economic growth or lost social welfare benefits that would accrue by waiting for the forecast revenue stream from the resource project to flow is greater than the interest cost of borrowing against that forecast revenue stream, then using an RFI model transaction to get the infrastructure built now and avoiding the delay is justified.

Infrastructure Pricing

Obtaining fair pricing of the infrastructure components in an RFI transaction can be a challenge for governments, particularly if the credit facility includes limitations on the sources of goods or services purchased with the loaned funds. There are two aspects of this issue: first, the quality of the infrastructure to be built; and second, the cost of that quality of infrastructure. Different prices for infrastructure can be compared only if the prices are offered for the same quality. The issue of pricing limitations due to use of a credit facility provided by a single lender is similar to the issue that arises in the traditional government infrastructure purchasing model, where concessional lending is "tied" to the purchase of goods and services from certain sources. This issue can pose even more of a challenge in an RFI transaction, however, since the government cannot "shop" for concessional funds with the least onerous restrictions.

In a project finance model transaction, when a government uses a competitive tender process that specifies the exact quality standards of the infrastructure to be built—or at least the quality of the outputs expected over the life of the project—the pricing is very transparent. Ideally, the pricing becomes the single parameter against which the winning bidder is selected. The price will reflect the cost of capital, including the equity investors' expected profits and the cost of loans; where concessional financing is available for the project, the value of the concessional lending will be passed through to the bid prices, but bidders will balance the use of available credit against any limitations on sourcing goods or services with that credit.

A government that is considering an RFI transaction should pay particular attention to any limitations imposed in the credit agreement that would restrict the government's ability to (i) specify the quality of the infrastructure it seeks, (ii) specify the identities of the contractors the government could invite to tender for the infrastructure construction or operations, or (iii) use a competitive process to get the best value for the money. In some cases the limitations may be unavoidable, at least for a portion of the credit facility.

As discussed above, there is a cost to a government when using an RFI credit to purchase infrastructure. Where the infrastructure is completed well in advance of the resource component producing revenues to service the debt, the additional accrued interest will inevitably increase the cost of the infrastructure, and reduce the amount of the credit facility that can be used for other components. Whether this cost is worth incurring depends on what the government's options are for alternative finance (either on a sovereign basis or through a PPP model or a project finance model transaction) and, as stated above, whether the value of the early availability of the infrastructure justifies the cost.

The cost of infrastructure under an RFI transaction, though somewhat higher than under a traditional government infrastructure purchasing model, may also reflect a "nonrecourse" benefit to the government. In a project finance model, if the project fails before the loans are repaid (and the government has not caused the failure due to, for example, failure to pay), the government typically does not have to repay the lenders to the project (or at least those lenders who have taken the project finance risk). Likewise, in the RFI model, the government commits a certain portion of the revenue stream from the resource component of the project for repayment of the debt. If the resource developer abandons the resource project after the government credit is drawn for infrastructure components (again, not due to government causes such as refusal to grant permits or approve imports of necessary equipment), then the government has no obligation to repay that credit from other sources. That is, the lender takes a "project risk" on the repayment of infrastructure loans, but this risk is the government's resource component revenue stream, not the revenues from the infrastructure facilities (if any). As in a project finance transaction, lenders will charge a premium for accepting this repayment risk, and governments need to determine whether this premium is worth the benefit of a non- or limited-recourse loan. An alternative approach would be to negotiate a credit agreement that looks to the government's resource component revenue stream as the primary source of repayment for the infrastructure component loans, but provides terms for sovereign repayment under perhaps a different repayment schedule should the resource component be delayed or cancelled—for example, if the target price for the resource declines by more than X percent for a period of Y years.

The Role of Concessional Finance

The use of concessional finance is a primary way governments of developing countries obtain infrastructure. For sovereign borrowing to enable government purchasing of infrastructure, the "concessions" include reduced credit standards for loan originations, extended repayment periods with long grace periods, and below-market interest rates frequently approaching 0 percent. In project finance and PPP transactions, the availability of concessional finance, whether direct to the project or on-lent through the government, can make projects "bankable," and reduce the costs of goods or services provided, as the low price of the concessional finance reduces the cost of the special purpose vehicle (SPV)'s capital.

From the available literature, it appears that most recent RFI-type transactions have involved the use of concessional finance, which has been used by the resource development company to initiate a resource development project, including the construction of associated infrastructure, and has been made available to the government for infrastructure construction against a pledge of the expected government revenue from the resource component. The availability of concessional finance to the resource developer makes remote (and thus expensive to obtain and export) resources economically viable to exploit at current forecast prices for the commodity, even when very substantial associated infrastructure investments are required.

It seems likely that where concessional finance is required to make the resource component of the RFI transaction financially viable, then concessional finance would be the only feasible source of funds for the credit to the government against the government's pledge of its forecast revenue stream from that project. This conclusion would be particularly strong in cases where concessional finance not only lowers the cost of resource exploitation (including the cost of constructing necessary associated infrastructure), but is an instrument of national economic security for the resource developer's country.

On the other hand, in the case of, say, a shallow-water, offshore oil production project, which could be financed through the development and production phases by one or more of the major oil companies using balance-sheet financing or commercial debt instruments, it seems likely that the government could obtain a commercial loan, or sell revenue bonds, against a pledge of part or all of its revenue stream from that project. This example would in effect result in an "unbundling" of the RFI transaction, leaving a stand-alone traditional resource development transaction and a linked RFI financing. The only involvement of the resource development investors would be to agree to pay the government's revenue stream into an escrow account established to service the credit facility.

By definition, the commercial debt instruments suggested in the prior paragraph would be more expensive (that is, have a higher interest rate payable) than concessional debt. Under the test where a government would use RFI financing only where the economic growth or social benefit has a higher value than the interest to be paid on the loan, the higher the interest rate on the RFI transaction credit facility, the higher the economic or social benefits must be to justify making the investment before the revenue stream is realized in due course. It may therefore be feasible in such cases to find ways to get concessional-priced credit facilities against a pledge of forecast future revenues from a resource project. The World Bank and other donors may be able to use their credit support instruments to reduce perceived risks of realizing the pledged revenue streams to lower the government's borrowing costs from the full commercial price. We suggest that this sort of hybrid "unbundled" approach can be further developed for specific transactions once the overall model is better understood and analyzed by relevant stakeholders.

Environmental and Social Obligations

Government laws and regulations regarding environmental and social requirements for both resource and infrastructure projects must be complied with by the developers and their contractors, regardless of the financing model used. The environmental and social issues in a resource component of an RFI project are as challenging as those in any other resource development project. These include resettlement issues for the area of the resource development project; the environmental risks of tailings or spills and other sources of air, water, and land pollution; and health and safety issues for both workers at the resource project and affected populations. Surety instruments to provide funds for mine or well decommissioning and closing costs are required for all resource development projects, including the resource development components of RFI projects. The need for governments to have sufficient staff and funds to effectively monitor and enforce environmental and social requirements over the life of the resource development and production period is as critical in an RFI project as in any other resource transaction.

There are also environmental and social obligations associated with infrastructure projects, regardless of the model used to structure the transaction. A government will need to establish these obligations, and then monitor compliance, for each infrastructure component of an RFI transaction—to the same extent as under a project finance transaction executed by a private developer, or under a government-owned infrastructure project built by a state-owned enterprise. The financing model used to fund an infrastructure project simply does not impact the environmental or social requirements that apply to the project.

Where government laws and regulations are deemed inadequate by international standards, development institutions and commercial lenders impose more stringent requirements. For example, for project finance and PPP model projects exceeding a minimum capital cost— that is, for virtually all infrastructure projects—participating international lenders will require compliance with the June 2013 "Equator Principles III," which incorporate World Bank Group environmental, social, health, and safety standards and guidelines where local laws would not require a project to meet these requirements. There may, however, be differences between the approaches taken by financial institutions that follow the Equator Principles and those national development finance institutions that look at projects from a national economic security point of view.

We suggest that the World Bank encourage all national development finance entities to follow the Equator Principles and adopt environmental and social best practices. Governments themselves may be at the forefront of requiring any foreign investor or contractor that wants to work in or profit from work in that country to adopt international norms on environmental and social issues, even if these standards are higher than those required by local laws. It makes little sense to undertake the effort to structure and negotiate an RFI transaction to accelerate economic growth and social welfare benefits, and then not require the developers and contractors to meet best practices on environmental and social obligations. A discussion of what those best practices are is beyond the scope of this study.

Donor entities could enter into a cofinancing program with the government, and offer to fund environmental and social components of infrastructure components of RFI projects, if those components cannot be covered by the government's credit facility from the RFI project. This approach would imply a level of transparency and cooperation that has not been evident in RFI transactions so far.

CHAPTER 6

Structural Issues

Key Contractual Arrangements in the Resource Financed Infrastructure Model

Each transaction, under any model, is defined by the contractual arrangements made among parties. The risks, rewards, and obligations are negotiated and agreed upon between parties. For many projects, the best approach is for the government to take the time, and make the effort, to define the project it wants, and to conduct a tender for that project with interested investors based on complete—or near-complete—documentation. The approach of using a competitive tender is well established for project finance transactions, and is becoming more common for public-private partnership (PPP) model projects. For direct government purchases of infrastructure, government compliance with procurement laws typically requires advertising and tendering for public contracts.

Best practices from all available models clearly suggest, therefore, that resource financed infrastructure (RFI) projects will be best structured, agreed on, and implemented when a comprehensive contracting approach is used. A government that is in the middle of the contractual arrangements for an RFI project will achieve the best results by considering separately the contracting arrangements for the resource, credit facility, and infrastructure components of the project.

From the perspective of the RFI model, the key unique contractual arrangement is the credit facility made available to the government, and the government's pledge of receivables from the resource development project as security for loans made under the credit facility. Other key contractual arrangements on the resource side include the resource development license and related documents, such as resource development plans, plans or contracts for associated infrastructure, and environmental and social mitigation commitments. For the infrastructure side, key contractual arrangements will vary depending on whether the government intends to own the infrastructure itself following construction, or intends to use a PPP approach that would involve a private sector party either as an operator as or an investor; the PPP partner could be either the resource development investor or another specialist entity. Robust tendering documents will ensure transparent and competitive contracts are achieved for the infrastructure components.

Experience to date has shown that early RFI transactions were approached on more of a "package deal" basis. Government-to-government "framework agreements" were put in place to guide the negotiations between the government and its state-owned resource development company on the one hand, and the investing country's state development bank and that country's interested resource development and infrastructure construction companies on the other hand. Such framework agreements to date have tended to limit opportunities for any competition between contractors for infrastructure components. Given the scope of an RFI transaction that includes large commitments of concessional funding by an investing country's state development bank, it is likely inevitable that there will be an intergovernmental framework agreement to establish the terms of negotiations for the various aspects of the transaction. Intergovernmental agreements are not, of course, tendered, nor are the negotiations on these items transparent.

When an intergovernmental framework agreement is contemplated, it is critical that the host-country government understand that its early commitments will establish a long-term precedent for everything else that happens under the RFI transaction. It is therefore very important that a host government seek qualified advisors early in the process, and not trust that the investing country's government is acting in the interest of the host government rather than of its own national interests. We also believe it is in the best interest of the investing country's government, and the investing country's state development bank and resource development and infrastructure construction companies, if it both encourages the host government to obtain qualified advisors early in the process, and has its own advisory team on board at the same time. The host government's advisory team need not be on board before introductory meetings, but should definitely be in place before the two sides start discussing term sheets or a memorandum of understanding (MOU), and certainly before negotiations for a draft framework agreement begin.

Tendering

The use of competitive tendering procedures allows a government to award contracts based on a transparent pricing mechanism: All other factors being equal, the best price wins. As suggested above, the basis for a successful tendering process is a set of clear and comprehensive bidding documents, including full drafts of relevant transaction contracts.

Tendering is most effective where the scope of a project is clear, and the scope of "known unknown" risks is manageable. Therefore, competitive tendering works very well for government procurement of buildings or road construction, and for project finance transactions involving proven technology, such as a gas-turbine power plant. Tendering is more difficult for projects that have, for example, unknown geotechnical conditions (such as the construction of a hydro-electric dam in an unstudied water basin) or where the contractor will be expected to use a novel or unproven technology to meet new needs (such as a contract to build a solar-thermal power plant of a size that has not yet been demonstrated).

From the government's point of view, tendering for the infrastructure components in an RFI project is especially important. The government is the party with the most interest in getting high-quality infrastructure at the most competitive prices possible. For the resource development component, the entity that holds the exploration rights for an area has the right to convert the exploration license to a development and production license pursuant to the terms of a resource law. The profitability of the development and production activities will depend on the resource developer purchasing high-quality facilities at the best possible prices. For the government credit facility component, tendering opportunities may be constrained if there is to be concessional financing, particularly if the concessional finance is provided by the same state development bank that finances the resource development component.

On the infrastructure component tendering issue, a government may seek to use the most transparent and competitive procedure possible, consistent with that country's procurement laws. The lessons learned from project finance transactions and the PPP model are directly applicable to tendering for infrastructure components in an RFI transaction when the government is contemplating any private sector involvement. When negotiating either an intergovernmental framework agreement or a credit agreement with a state development bank, the host government can negotiate strongly to obtain the most open, transparent, and competitive procurement procedures possible for use of the government credit facility, including involvement of third-party private investors should the government choose to use a PPP model structure for one or more of those investments. Rather than limit infrastructure construction firms allowed to be paid from the government credit facility to those from the state development bank's country, it may be possible to negotiate the use of a tendering process that provides a small preference at the prequalification stage to contractors from the development bank's country, or that reserves perhaps two or three places on the prequalified bidder list for companies from that country that meet the minimum qualification standards.

As an alternative, if the state development agency or investing country government requires that all infrastructure built with the government's credit facility be sourced (both goods and services) from the investing country, then another approach would be for the host government to choose the types of infrastructure for which the investing country has excellent contractors. This consideration should be in the mind of the host government before starting negotiations on any part of an RFI transaction, in particular an MOU or a framework agreement.

Structure of Contract Liabilities and Settlement of Disputes, Current Practices, Main Issues, and Options

The first observation from experience under all transaction models is that allocating contract liabilities works best, and prices are lowest, when contract rights and liabilities are allocated between the parties according to an agreed risk allocation approach. Each risk is typically allocated to the party best able to mitigate it, whether by controlling its own activities or by insuring the risk or passing the risk on to another contractor.

For example, in a construction contract under most transaction structures, if the government requires a building to be completed by, say, July 1, then it will ask the building developer to commit to complete the building by July 1 (or somewhat sooner to allow for contingencies). If the developer receives assurance from its suppliers and subcontractors that it can complete the building on time, then the developer will commit to the government that it can complete the building, and will agree to pay damages to the government if the building is completed late. The developer, in turn, will seek to recover those damages from its suppliers and contractors should any of them be the cause of a late completion. But the developer will also try to avoid liability for late completion damages, and seek damages of its own from the government, if the government causes the developer to be late by, for example, failing to make the site available on time (if the site was a government responsibility); failing to make timely progress payments, according to the contract; failing to provide building permits or inspections on a timely basis; or failing to clear project building supplies or equipment through border checkpoints in a timely manner. The developer will also purchase insurance against poor weather and loss of supplies during shipment, either directly or through the terms of supply and transportation agreements. The cost of these insurances will be in the contract price the government pays for the building, but those costs are the price of the performance the government requires. The risks, once identified, are therefore allocated to the appropriate party and drafted into—and priced as part of—the project contracts.

In the RFI context the same approach to identifying and allocating risks would be used. The key is for the parties to identify and allocate risks not just on two sides of the transaction, but between the government and each of the resource developer, the credit facility provider, and the infrastructure developers or contractors. The resource developer, credit facility provider, and infrastructure developers or contractors will also likely have agreements among themselves, to further allocate risks. When additional parties are involved (such as contractors for associated infrastructure construction, private sector investors in the infrastructure components, or other engineering, procurement, and construction [EPC] contractors), the number of required agreements will be higher.

The resource development license and related documents can incorporate best practices from the traditional resource development model projects, and the infrastructure construction contracts (whether structured similarly to a traditional government infrastructure purchasing transaction or to a PPP or project finance model transaction) may incorporate all applicable best practices from those models.

The key distinguishing attribute of the RFI model is that the loan the government obtains to purchase infrastructure is paid back directly from the government revenues associated with the resource development component and pledged to the entity that made the loan. Put simply, the government is buying infrastructure with its own money, albeit on a nonrecourse basis. A government can take all steps necessary to ensure the investment of its funds are done efficiently, as with any project where a government is procuring infrastructure in its own name, and to obtain maximum value for its citizens, including by hiring additional qualified staff or consultants, if needed, to undertake the procurement and construction supervision processes in a professional manner. Governments can avoid the risk of not taking "ownership" of the process to ensure that the infrastructure is tendered and contracted for appropriately, and follow through to ensure that the infrastructure contractor's performance is in accordance with contract requirements.

The main issue is for all stakeholders to understand and acknowledge that the infrastructure components of RFI transactions are not "gifts" from the investing country's development bank (even when concessional finance is offered), and are not "free" simply because the loan taken for the infrastructure construction is to be paid back directly by the resource development licensee. Governments and all stakeholders must understand that in an RFI transaction a government is buying the infrastructure with its own money, through the pledge of the government's right to a future revenue stream from the resource development component. Seen in this light, a host government has every right to insist that its money, or rather the money it is managing on behalf of the citizens of that country, is used efficiently, transparently, and to obtain good value that endures over time. Moreover, it is not appropriate to consider the resource and infrastructure components of an RFI transaction as "swaps" for each other, as though a government has no option as to the infrastructure it wants, or no rights to enforce performance obligations of an infrastructure contractor. The more appropriate option is to see an RFI transaction as primarily a financing mechanism to link a resource component with the early development of infrastructure, through a credit facility supported by the pledge of a revenue stream.

Sharing of Risk

Development of any kind of project, under every model, is an exercise in sharing risks. The development of risk-sharing mechanisms in an RFI transaction follows the same pattern, albeit using a combination of a resource development component and one or more infrastructure procurement components. Contracts and other project documents are the means by which the risk-sharing allocations are recorded, and these documents may be structured and negotiated separately for each component, while recognizing the inherent interconnections between the resource and infrastructure components that exist because of the financing links. For an RFI transaction, as in every transaction under every model, an appropriate sharing of risks is to allocate each risk to the party best able to bear it, and to provide incentives (typically penalties in the form of agreed liquidated damages) if that party does not manage the risk to an acceptable, agreed-upon level.

Under the RFI model, the resource developer will take the risk that it will complete the resource extraction project on time and on budget, and ultimately that the resource is available at the "proven" levels and can be extracted, processed, and exported at costs that provide an opportunity for profits. Governments will not, except in the most extreme and unusual circumstances, guarantee the existence of the resource nor the overall profitability of the resource project. The resource developer will not, under normal circumstances, be liable to repay any loans advanced to the host government if the government revenue stream pledged to secure the government credit facility proves inadequate. The resource developer may, however, be required to pay interest costs above the amount capitalized in the government loan if the reason the additional interest accrues is because the resource development was late or over budget, thereby causing a shortfall from the revenue stream agreed on at the time the credit facility was signed. This approach would be consistent with the approach of a project finance model, where late completion or other poor performance affects the profitability of the project investors. The resource developer will not normally be held responsible for late or inadequate completion of the infrastructure components (except to the extent the resource developer is also involved in the infrastructure component). To the extent its late completion of the resource component delays repayment of the government's infrastructure credit, however, the resource developer could reasonably take on the risk of additional accrued interest.

The resource developer would not, in most circumstances, take risks associated with the infrastructure components of an RFI transaction, unless the resource developer is also a partner in a PPP-type structure or is part of an infrastructure construction contract consortium, and thereby a party to one or more infrastructure component contracts. Where the resource and infrastructure contractors are separate entities, the only link the resource developer would have with the infrastructure component is to pay the government's pledged revenue stream to the debt service account for the government's credit facility. If the infrastructure component goes overbudget, is completed late, or otherwise is not satisfactory or even fails, the resource developer will remain unaffected so long as it continues to perform satisfactorily under its development and production licenses. On the other hand, where an intergovernmental framework agreement is used that explicitly links the performance of the infrastructure contractors to the continued rights of the resource developer to continue development and production activities, a different result could occur. This alternative may be warranted where the government is required to use infrastructure contractors nominated by the development bank as a condition of the government credit facility.

Where the government will own the infrastructure built with proceeds from the credit facility directly, or through a state-owned agency, the risk allocation between the government and the infrastructure construction contractors would be virtually the same as in any other contract under a traditional government infrastructure purchasing transaction. The government may require compliance with construction standards, and have the right to supervise construction and receive periodic reports, including test reports on materials used in the construction. Payments will be made on achieving defined construction milestones, perhaps with a retainer against completion and satisfaction of final completion tasks. Normal industry warranties will be provided in favor of the government, as owner, and liquidated damages will be due for deviations from project specifications or timelines. Where performance does not meet minimum acceptable standards, and the contractor does not remedy the situation, the government may have the right to reject the nonconforming components; or, where the nonconforming components make the entire project unsafe or unusable, it may reject the entire project.

A significant feature of the RFI model is the risk allocation of the entity providing the credit facility to the government. Under a project finance model contract, the lender would have a strong interest in monitoring the construction and operations and maintenance (O&M) of the infrastructure built using loan proceeds, because successful operation of that infrastructure would be the sole source of revenues to repay the loan. Thus, in a project finance transaction, the government may at least partially rely on the lender's consultants (and the equity investor's consultants) to monitor performance by the infrastructure construction company. In an RFI transaction, by contrast, the lender looks to the pledged government revenue stream from the resource component of the transaction for repayment of its loan, so the amount of effort the lender may commit to supervising construction of the infrastructure is likely to be significantly diminished. Therefore, in an RFI transaction, the government must be prepared to undertake the full role of ensuring that the infrastructure component is properly specified in the construction contract, and properly built. As discussed in the next subsection, this government risk may be mitigated by adopting features of the PPP model for the infrastructure components.

An alternative risk allocation approach for a government to consider when negotiating an RFI transaction credit facility with the lender would arise where (i) a national development finance entity is involved, and (ii) the national development finance entity requires, as a condition of agreeing to the credit facility, that the government use one (or a limited number) of suppliers of goods and services for the infrastructure construction components. The more restrictive the credit facility is on the use of the proceeds, the more risk the development finance entity should take if the result of those restrictions is that the infrastructure components are over budget, late, or of poor quality. Under the RFI model, no matter how poorly the infrastructure is built (and complaints about poor infrastructure are one of the main criticisms of existing RFI arrangements), the lending agency is assured of full repayment so long as the resource component is successful. Assigning more risk to the lending agency would cause it to act more like a lender to a project finance model transaction (for example, additional risk might cause the loan costs to increase), even though repayment of the loan would be from the resource component, which may not start producing revenues for up to 10 years. Exactly how to implement this sort of risk allocation will depend on the circumstances of each project.

Resource Financed Infrastructure • http://dx.doi.org/10.1596/978-1-4648-0239-3

Government Ownership/Joint Ventures

The issue of whether a government will have an ownership interest, or exercise a "right of participation," either directly or through a state-owned enterprise, raises different concerns in the resource and infrastructure components of the RFI model. These concerns are the same a government would face on the resource side of a traditional resource development project, and on the infrastructure side of a project finance or PPP model transaction. In the traditional government infrastructure purchasing model, of course, the government takes a full-ownership interest in the infrastructure that it acquires. Whether a government takes an ownership interest in an RFI transaction may be considered separately for the resource and infrastructure components. When an RFI transaction has several infrastructure projects financed from the credit facility, the government can also choose to take full, partial, or no-ownership interest in each project, depending on what makes the most sense to fulfill the government's objectives in that project.

For the resource component, whether the government has an ownership interest will be decided in the same way as for any other resource production project in the country. If the resource development law for hydrocarbons or metal ore, for example, allows a state resource entity to exercise a right of participation either to "buy in" or to reserve a "free carry" for each project, then those requirements would apply equally to the resource component of an RFI transaction. Such government ownership interests provide an additional forecast revenue stream (to royalties, income taxes, and other taxes and license fees) that the government could pledge to secure the credit facility that would facilitate the infrastructure component of the RFI project.

For the infrastructure component, as discussed above, the infrastructure investments that are part of an RFI transaction can be structured as 100 percent government contracted and owned facilities, as in a traditional government infrastructure purchasing model, or with the characteristics of any of the PPP-type structures, including those that look very similar to the project finance model (except for the essential requirement that forecasted cash flows from the project will pay for the project).

A government may want to consider bringing the private sector into an infrastructure component of an RFI transaction, for the same reasons it would decide to involve the private sector in a project finance or PPP transaction:

- To have another private party with specialized expertise who would have an incentive to ensure that the infrastructure construction contractor is performing as required
- To have an operator on hand during construction to ensure that the new facilities are used correctly and efficiently as construction is completed
- To bring additional capital (or to employ additional donor funds) to provide any facilities not covered under the infrastructure construction contract

A private partner involved in the O&M of the infrastructure facility could be unrelated to the contractor building the infrastructure facility. For example, in a case where the government draws on an RFI transaction credit facility to build a new hospital, the government may separately tender for a hospital operator to take over the outfitting of the building with equipment and staff, and the operations of the hospital for a period of, say, 10 years. The hospital operator may take an ownership interest in the hospital and the funds it injects would be used to purchase fixtures and supplies, and hire and pay staff. Part of the hospital operator's mandate could also be to supervise construction of the facility to ensure that all sanitary requirements, systems, and other components to be supplied by the infrastructure contractor are properly completed.

The example in the previous paragraph is intended to indicate the approaches that could be used to access expertise and other funds to integrate new infrastructure purchased with RFI transaction government credit facilities. Other approaches include involving the resource developer and/or the infrastructure construction contractor as joint-venture partner(s) in the infrastructure component. The appropriate approach to be used for specific RFI transactions, or parts of RFI transactions, will depend on the government's priorities and objectives for each component.

CHAPTER 7

Operational Issues

The resource financed infrastructure (RFI) model contains within it incentives to ensure that the infrastructure components are built to specified standards, and that long-term operations and maintenance (O&M) plans and budgets are adequately prepared and adopted. These incentives are based on a proper understanding that the owner of property (who is paying for the property) has an incentive to maintain that property to get the most economic value from it over time. Where an RFI transaction will result in a government owning the infrastructure, then—as in the traditional government infrastructure purchasing model—the government obtains that infrastructure with its own funds (albeit borrowed from future revenue streams). As the owner of the assets, the government has the incentive to take every precaution to ensure high quality and a good price. Where the infrastructure assets of an RFI transaction would be owned and/or operated through a public-private partnership (PPP) model structure, then both the government and the private partner would have incentives to maintain the infrastructure, as in any other PPP transaction.

That the RFI model, like other models, provides the proper incentives does not, however, mean that these incentives are properly captured in specific transactions, or that even if a transaction is structured correctly, the implementation of the project will be effective. Unfortunately, many projects under all project models have fallen short. The limited experience to date with RFI transactions has resulted in criticism on the grounds that the infrastructure built has crumbled very quickly, particularly in the case of road projects.

These criticisms of early RFI transactions tend to show that the stakeholders in these projects may not have adequately prepared for the period after which the infrastructure was completed, even if the construction contracts were well specified and properly managed. There is a special risk in RFI transactions that does not exist in project finance transactions, or even most PPP transactions, because the lender is looking for repayment of the loans for the infrastructure components from the pledged resource revenue stream. Criticism of poor infrastructure construction where the government will own the assets is not unique to RFI transactions; poor construction occurs all too often where a government obtains infrastructure through tied aid. Many projects, especially "vanity" projects "donated" to countries by foreign governments, or built in anticipation of a specific event (for example, a regional summit meeting or soccer tournament), tend to suffer from poor construction quality and premature deterioration.

We believe that governments and other stakeholders that properly understand the RFI model will recognize the incentives within each RFI transaction to ensure success in the operational phases of the project. Listed below are the key operational issues for stakeholders to consider and address before embarking on an RFI transaction.

Quality of the Infrastructure/Third-Party Supervision

The issue of quality construction and the need for independent supervision and monitoring of construction, environmental, and social requirements applies just as strongly to transactions under the RFI model as to transactions under every other model. The party with the strongest motivation to perform these functions does, however, differ slightly across models.

For example, in a project finance or PPP model transaction, especially where the revenues from the project will be the sole source of funds to repay debt, the special purpose vehicle (SPV) owner and the lender will both have strong incentives to supervise the construction process. For major projects, each will typically have its own consulting engineers—known as the "owner's engineer" and "lender's engineer"—who will closely supervise all aspects of the construction process. The construction contractors will be entitled to milestone payments only after both engineers agree that the materials used and work performed has met the required standards.

For the resource component of an RFI transaction, the resource developer is as strongly motivated to ensure compliance with all requirements as in any traditional resource development transaction. These include environmental, labor, and other general legal requirements, in addition to resource development and production license requirements, including the payment of applicable royalties and taxes. Persistent failure to comply with the legal and license requirements associated with the development and production of the resource can lead to revocation of the resource production license, and therefore loss of the investment (and of course the expected profits).

Lenders to a resource developer also are strongly motivated to ensure compliance with requirements, and will frequently hire third-party consultants to monitor performance throughout the duration of the loan for the resource component. To the extent the lender has also extended the credit facility for the government's purchase of infrastructure, the lender will be even more motivated to ensure the resource development component complies with requirements and performs well.

The government, in its role as the resource production regulator, will have a clear obligation to monitor and enforce license terms; the construction, environmental, social, and other legal requirements; and the correct calculation of royalties attributable to the government under the resource production license. The government as tax collector likewise has an incentive to enforce the applicable tax regime, and through its ownership of any state-owned resource enterprise (that is, a partner or joint owner of the resource project) an incentive to ensure that those rights are also protected and enforced.

For the infrastructure component of an RFI transaction, the government must take the primary responsibility for construction supervision. As discussed above, the lender for the infrastructure investment will look for repayment to the committed government revenue stream from the resource component, so it has little incentive to enforce quality standards beyond ensuring that loan disbursements are made in good faith upon submission of the relevant documents evincing milestone achievements.

Quality assurance in infrastructure projects requires specialist knowledge and skills relating to the particular type of project, so to the extent a government does not have personnel with the expertise to supervise the construction directly, the government may hire a consulting firm unrelated to, and preferably from a different country than, the primary contractor building the infrastructure. If these quality-assurance consultants cannot be hired under the government credit agreement as part of the RFI project, then the government may seek funds from other sources for this purpose. Failure to undertake diligent quality-assurance steps almost inevitably leads to poor results, so although it may seem expensive, quality-assurance work is a necessary expense to ensure the government receives value for the resource revenue stream it has committed.

There are alternate options available to ensure adequate construction supervision. One option is for a government to use a PPP structure for the operational phase of the infrastructure facility, and require that the private partner be responsible for performing quality assurance during the construction phase (directly or by hiring a quality-assurance consulting firm). Another option is to shift part of the risk back to the lender, particularly where the lender imposes limitations on the government's choice of infrastructure construction companies, perhaps by waiving repayment of part or all of the related government credit to the extent it becomes evident that an infrastructure component was not completed in accordance with the required standards. This step would at least partially align the lender's interests with the government's, in that the lender would have an incentive to hire a lender's engineer, and may result in the contractor agreeing to liquidated damages for poor performance where it was otherwise unwilling to do so. In essence, the repayment of the loan would be contingent on the continuing performance of the infrastructure even though the revenue for repayment would come from the pledged resource revenue stream. Over time, however, it may become difficult to determine whether an infrastructure project deteriorated prematurely because of poor construction, or poor ongoing maintenance.

Regardless of the option, or mix of options, used in an RFI transaction to ensure that infrastructure components are constructed according to the agreed-upon standards, the key considerations for the parties in the negotiation process are to ensure that the specifications for the infrastructure component are properly set forth from the beginning—this step may require the government to obtain independent consultant participation if it does not have the expertise available internally—and to ensure that the warranty coverage, including damages payable, are appropriate for the type of infrastructure facility built.

Operation and Maintenance of Infrastructure

O&M is key for most infrastructure projects, whether in developing countries or developed countries. In a project finance infrastructure project, the private investor is motivated, together with the project lenders, to ensure that facilities are operated and maintained appropriately throughout the life of the investment; if the facilities fail, the project stops producing revenue and both the lenders and equity investors lose. PPP model transactions may shield the investors from part of the losses upon project failure, and impose losses on the government as a partner in the project. In traditional government infrastructure purchasing transactions, it is unfortunate that many developing country governments have less problem raising donor and export credit agency financing for new infrastructure, or for major rehabilitation of failed infrastructure, than for prudent ongoing maintenance activities.

In an RFI transaction, the credit facility, based on the pledge of the government's forecast revenue stream from the resource component, is used to purchase infrastructure, but because the lender will look to the resource component for repayment, the lender may not focus on the long-term sustainability of the infrastructure facilities. The government is therefore responsible for ensuring the facilities it buys with the credit facility are operated and maintained to provide overall value to the country, just as in a traditional government infrastructure purchasing transaction.

One option to improve this situation would be to use additional portions of the credit facility from the resource component of an RFI project to purchase a multiyear O&M contract from a private O&M company, perhaps an affiliate of the construction contractor (essentially making the infrastructure facility a PPP-type activity). This approach could be used for any number of infrastructure projects, such as school or hospital buildings, water or wastewater treatment projects, or road projects. The term of the O&M contract could be until the government is likely to have uncommitted revenues available from the resource project—or from any other source—sufficient to make O&M payments on an ongoing basis. This approach would impair the use of the credit facility by the cost of the O&M contract during the term, but would ensure sustainability of the investment and may improve the warranty terms on offer from the construction contractor if the contractor's affiliate is hired for the O&M contract.

Another option is for the government to use the entire credit facility as soon as possible for infrastructure construction projects, and find alternate funding sources (including donor grants/loans, private sector partners, or others) to pay for certain categories of O&M costs. This option would work best where the infrastructure facility is expected to produce some revenues—say, revenues sufficient for ongoing salary costs—but not revenues sufficient to pay for other O&M costs to maintain the physical plant or renew equipment and supplies.

In any event, separating the O&M component of the infrastructure project from the tender for the construction of the infrastructure facility is another way to increase transparency and competition in an RFI transaction, particularly if the terms of the credit facility are such that a government's options for tendering the original construction competitively are limited.

Specification of Technical Standards and Monitoring Requirements

In every project, under every model, the government must specify clear technical standards before construction begins, and before negotiation of the construction contracts. The choice of the standards for a project will have a direct impact on the cost of the project. Agreeing on the standards for both the infrastructure and resource components of the RFI project—and, in particular, the environmental and social requirements—is as important while negotiating an RFI transaction as any other, from traditional government infrastructure purchasing transactions to project finance transactions.

Potential investors in RFI transactions (including a government that initiates a framework agreement on a resource developer's behalf) may propose what at first seems a "done deal" with no or few specifications of construction standards and little room for negotiation. Host-country governments, meanwhile, are responsible for negotiating these transactions to ensure that the infrastructure to be built meets local requirements. A government must keep in mind at all times that the infrastructure components are being built with the government's own money, albeit accelerated from a future revenue stream to a current loan.

Box 7.1 Choosing Standards

The question of which standards to use for a particular project does not have a straightforward answer. Using an inappropriate standard can result in inappropriate infrastructure. For example, if the standard chosen for constructing a power plant requires expensive measures for earthquake protection, but the area where the power plant will be built is not seismically active, then the cost of the power plant will be too high. Conversely, if a contract for a road project contains standards that do not reflect the subsurface conditions of the area where the road will be built, or do not reflect the types of truck traffic that will use the road, then the cost of the project will be low, but the road will likely fail very quickly. Thus, it is not necessary to use the most stringent standards in every case, but to use—and then enforce—standards appropriate to the specific project.

Developing standards, and then updating them over time, is an expensive regulatory burden. Another country's standards may be adopted after careful consideration, and when appropriate for a specific project can save time and money. There are widely accepted industry

box continues next page

Resource Financed Infrastructure · http://dx.doi.org/10.1596/978-1-4648-0239-3

Box 7.1 Choosing Standards *(continued)*

standards, too, such as the FIDIC construction contracts developed by the International Federation of Consulting Engineers, or the IEEE standards developed by the Institute of Electrical and Electronics Engineers. These standards often have alternate provisions, with elections to be made depending on the specific circumstances of each project. The advantage of using internationally accepted standards is that many suppliers and developers are familiar with them, allowing a more competitive tender and reducing the cost of supervision and quality assurance. The standards used must, even in the case of those that are internationally accepted, be appropriate for the government's specific project needs.

Likewise, the government is responsible for monitoring the construction and operations of infrastructure facilities built through RFI transactions, just as it must monitor every other construction contract for which it is the purchaser under a traditional government infrastructure purchasing transaction. The resource investor (and its lender) can be relied on to supervise the construction of the resource component facilities, including associated infrastructure, to ensure the facilities meet technical requirements, but even for those components the government also has a right—and obligation—to supervise construction to ensure compliance with all applicable environmental and social requirements, in addition to compliance with applicable construction codes.

If a government does not have experts available who can adequately monitor either the infrastructure or resource construction or operation activities, or the technical, environmental, social, or other aspects, specialist consultants may be hired. The costs of these consultants may be paid directly from government funds, from funds made available by other donors, or by use of the credit facility made available under the RFI transaction. Governments could consider what portions of the reports of the expert compliance monitors (to the extent confidential information is not included) to make public, to increase the transparency of transactions and reduce public skepticism. The value of transparency is heightened if the monitors discover problems in the construction or operation of any part of the RFI transaction facilities; public acknowledgment of a problem and the steps that are to be undertaken to solve it will improve public perception of both the project itself and the government's role in the project.

CHAPTER 8

Conclusions

As we have seen, the resource financed infrastructure (RFI) model was developed as a way to meet the needs of investors and governments. Governments of resource-rich, developing countries want to obtain essential infrastructure to improve the lives of their populations and grow their economies; resource developers who have found promising deposits of valuable hydrocarbons, ore, or other resources want to invest in the development and production of these resources to earn profits. The RFI model connects the resource development activity to the government's accelerated access to infrastructure by use of an innovative financing mechanism.

In hindsight, the implementation of early projects that can be deemed to have used variants of the RFI model has not been ideal, as evidenced by press and academic criticism of those projects. But we believe that a significant part of the perceived implementation problems may reflect an improper understanding of the RFI model—among both stakeholders and critics—as a form of "swap" or "barter" rather than a new form of financing.

The authors of this study see great value in the RFI model, in particular as a way to accelerate development in infrastructure through pledging, in a limited-recourse way, future government revenues from a resource development project. Concessional finance has been used for these transactions to date, in particular from the home country of the resource developer, but we see scope for other donors and finance institutions to invest or lend in parallel with an RFI project to leverage the value of the project for the country by improving competitiveness, sustainability, and environmental and social factors.

There are many important—and related—financial, structural, and operational issues for stakeholders to consider before embarking on negotiations for an RFI model transaction. Most of these issues are common to any transaction under any model, in any country. The resolution of the issues, however, must be tailored to the specific transaction, and the specific interests and policies of the participants to the transaction.

We have written this study not as a way to settle the issues discussed above, but to begin a discussion among stakeholders on a new and potentially very useful way to finance infrastructure projects in the developing world. Interested parties who may become involved in an RFI transaction can consider the short-comings of experiences under the RFI model to date to create and implement better transactions in the future.

We look forward to the discussion.

PART 3

Comments

Paul Collier
Co-Director, Centre for the Study of African Economies, Oxford University
Professor of Economics and Public Policy, Blavatnik School of Government, Oxford University

Alan Gelb
Senior Fellow, Center for Global Development
Former World Bank Chief Economist for Africa

Justin Yifu Lin
Honorary Dean of the National School of Development, Peking University
Former Chief Economist of the World Bank

The Rt. Hon. Clare Short
Chair, Extractive Industries Transparency Initiative

Yan Wang
Visiting Professor, George Washington University

Louis T. Wells
Herbert F. Johnson Professor Emeritus, Harvard Business School

Comments by Paul Collier

Co-Director, Centre for the Study of African Economies, Oxford University

Professor of Economics and Public Policy, Blavatnik School of Government, Oxford University

This is a useful study, but it is written from a legal perspective rather than an economic one. I will make five economic points.

First, linking resource extraction to infrastructure is a *commitment technology*. If I were in the position of a prudent finance minister, I would find this aspect of the deals rather attractive. If, instead, the minister follows the standard international finance institution (IFI) advice and sells the natural resource, taking the revenues into the budget, this indeed preserves flexibility as to what to spend on, but such flexibility need not be desirable. Ministers responsible for depleting their natural assets need a commitment technology to ensure that future decision takers devote a sensible proportion of these unsustainable revenues to the accumulation of assets (of whatever type). Typically, a finance minister has no such commitment technology: by the time the revenues arrive, he might well not even be finance minister, and even if he is, his views might not prevail in a cabinet facing pressures for recurrent spending. The pressure to use resource revenues for recurrent spending has increased with contested elections: governments' time horizons have shortened just when resource discoveries make it important that their horizons should lengthen. By signing away the prospective revenues to finance infrastructure, the government achieves this precommitment. Of course, it is not the first-best option. First-best option would be an asset commitment technology that left the choice of assets more open. But it might be the best choice available.

Second, the opaque nature of infrastructure-for-resources (resources for infrastructure [RfI] hereafter) deals is indeed worrisome. But the key reason for this is that there is a monopoly situation in the supply of such deals. If there were several package deal providers—for example, if bilateral donors teamed up with their national resource companies and construction companies—then the value of RfI deals could be determined through competition even if internally they remained opaque. This may be a more realistic approach than trying to make the deals more transparent. Governments would then be able to initiate bidding processes for the infrastructure they wanted, rather than face *ad hoc* unsolicited offers as at present.

Third, an important reason why governments find these deals attractive is their speed. The study emphasizes the speedy provision of finance (as opposed to waiting for revenues to flow), but another key reason why they are fast is that they bypass the cumbersome procedures with which the IFIs have festooned their provision of finance for infrastructure. Environmental impact assessments, procurement procedures, and suchlike have been designed with good intentions, but the impetus for them has not been the expressed demand of African governments but the lobbying of Western nongovernmental organizations. I suspect that these procedures have accumulated to the point at which they are dysfunctional even in their own terms because they induce the total bypass provided by RfI deals in their current form. The IFIs have to find ways of radically streamlining their procedures to fit the expressed requirements of African governments, otherwise they will become irrelevant for Africa's infrastructure investment process.

Fourth, whereas the scope of the study is explicitly limited to infrastructure functionally unrelated to the extraction project, the infrastructure provided in these deals can be of two types. Some of it is unrelated to the needs of resource extraction—as when the country gets an airport in return for ore. Other infrastructure is provided because it is necessary for resource extraction. The latter raises important issues of how other potential users are catered to. Governments should usually insist that infrastructure for resource extraction should be designed to be both multiuser (that is, involving other resource extraction companies) and multifunction (that is, ensuring the carriage of freight other than resources). However, the devil with such a requirement is in the detail of pricing. For example, a railway has very high fixed costs, so that marginal costs are far lower than average costs. An efficient use of the infrastructure needed for resource extraction requires that the fixed costs be covered by the natural resource freight, leaving nonresource users paying only a marginal cost. This needs to be written into the regulatory structure agreed on at the point of contracting. The government has to represent the interest of prospective nonresource users.

Finally, consider some infrastructure (such as a power station), the construction of which is financed through the government pledging future resource revenues. Whereas the negotiation and construction phases of infrastructure such as a power station have often proved too fraught for project finance (which is why the pledging of resource revenues is necessary), once it is built and running it becomes a relatively low-risk utility. At this stage the government could on-sell the infrastructure to a private operator. Such a deal does not need to be agreed on at the time of the RfI deal, but it should be preserved as an option to be exercised. In a capital-scarce, high-risk environment, governments should not be tying up their limited capital in low-risk, capital-intensive infrastructure that could be operated privately. Used in this way, the pledging of resource revenues is useful collateral to unblock the obstacles that have frustrated project finance in difficult environments.

Resource Financed Infrastructure • http://dx.doi.org/10.1596/978-1-4648-0239-3

Comments by Alan Gelb

Senior Fellow, Center for Global Development
Former World Bank Chief Economist for Africa

The resource financed infrastructure (RFI) approach has generated a great deal of controversy, and the study performs a valuable service in laying out the approach in a systematic way, and drawing on several other approaches to explain what new it brings to the table. As the study explains, there are three components: the resource side involving the terms for generating future revenue flows, the structuring of a loan agreement secured by part of the stream of resource revenues, and the use of the funds to advance infrastructure investments in advance of the actual receipt of resource revenues. This enables the host country to mortgage part of its future revenues to speed up its development plans in a way that might otherwise not be possible.

The study makes useful distinctions between the principles underlying the RFI model and past practices in implementing it, arguing that faults in implementation do not necessarily invalidate the good points of the approach. In particular, it makes a strong case for increased transparency, which will also help to improve understanding of the RFI approach, as being more than a swap of resources for infrastructure. If the initial transactions had been implemented in a transparent way, the approach might indeed have generated less controversy and concern. As the study observes, all approaches have their strengths and weaknesses, so that many of the objections that can be levied against the RFI model can also apply to other approaches. But there are still questions about the likely incentives in this type of contract, including some that seem to push against transparency.

The first test for potential RFI is the nature of the advantage obtained from securitizing future resource revenue flows. It is not clear from the study how this would enhance the credit of a high-risk government that was not able to contract sovereign debt. Would Zimbabwe, for example, enhance its credit by pledging revenues from its Marenge diamonds? What additional security is provided to the lender over and above that to any sovereign creditor? If little, one would expect an RFI loan to be available from an "arm's-length" lender only at a high cost.

The study also appears to assume that other lenders, such as the International Monetary Fund (IMF) or a multilateral development bank (MDB), which might have conditions to limit the assumption of more sovereign debt, will sit passively on the sidelines while the government pledges a part of its future resource revenues. This does not seem realistic. Even if the country were able to contract more debt by pledging future resource taxes, this would further downgrade creditworthiness for other creditors and other borrowing, and hence have a cost to the country that is additional to the cost of the infrastructure loan.

The second test for RFI is whether such an arrangement could still be attractive if each of the three components were negotiated separately and with full disclosure. This does not seem to have been the case so far. The study recognizes that all RFI contracts are likely to involve linkages between the three components, and that this will inevitably work against transparency (for example, the most likely lender is an entity that is familiar with the resource developments). It notes a number of factors that might encourage linkages between the resource company, the lender, and the infrastructure providers, including a possible strategic interest in an importing country obtaining access to the resources themselves. Without these linkages, the full costs of advancing infrastructure spending for a less-than-creditworthy resource producer might be very high, especially if the lender prices in risk fully. With the linkages, and without full transparency on each of the three components, the RFI transaction becomes extremely complex, making it far more difficult for outsiders to understand and monitor the costs and benefits of the deal, and weakening parliamentary oversight of the government's fiscal commitments. It is not clear that the lack of transparency in existing cases is an accident or due to a failure to understand the instrument.

There are therefore still some questions on exactly how the RFI model overcomes imperfections in the credit markets and whether the model would be viable under transparent, arm's-length conditions.

The study makes an interesting suggestion on the use of concessional funds from official lenders to lower the cost of credit extended against future-pledged revenue streams. This could take various forms, for example, an interest-rate buy-down or a partial risk guarantee against the government reneging on the agreement. For this to be viable, the RFI transaction would need to be highly transparent, including in all three components and preferably including procurement. Some countries are moving in this direction, and it would be useful to study their experience.

A caution not sufficiently stressed by the study is the bad historical record of huge, accelerated, investment booms in a range of resource-exporting countries. These are most severe when an influx of resources enables investment to be scaled up very rapidly, far in advance of the systems needed to manage it well. This introduces an additional layer of caution when considering the RFI model.

On the other side, the study also does not seem to note one important defense of the approach. At least the resource-producing country will receive some infrastructure for its resources, compared to a possible alternative scenario where revenues either fail to be included in the budget or, once there, are wasted or stolen. RFI can also be seen as a precommitment mechanism, limiting the ability of a successor government from raiding a large sovereign wealth fund.

Comments by Justin Yifu Lin* and Yan Wang**

*Honorary Dean of the National School of Development, Peking University, and Former Chief Economist of the World Bank

**Visiting Professor, George Washington University

The world economy needs a growth-lifting strategy, and infrastructure financing seems to hold the key.[1] As we think about long-term financing for the post-2015 era, this research effort initiated by the World Bank, aiming to better evaluate the resource financed infrastructure (RFI hereafter) approach, is timely. The study provides a framework to evaluate the strengths and weaknesses of various contractual arrangements for infrastructure financing, including the RFI approach. It is pertinent, objective, and well researched. This analytic initiative should continue.

The authors are right to highlight the time dimension of the RFI approach by pointing out that it "can bring substantial benefits to a [host] country and its citizens,... **years ahead** of what would have been possible under any other model," but the study says relatively little about the "structural" side of the analysis. Based on the intellectual foundation of New Structural Economics (Lin 2012), we would like to stress the developmental aspects of the RFI concept, especially focusing on the "structural," the "currency," and the "spatial" dimensions, as well as political economy and transparency issues, while leaving the evaluation of past RFI transactions to further analysis.

First, economic development is a process of continuous industrial and technological upgrading in which each country, regardless of its level of development, can succeed if it develops industries that are consistent with its comparative advantage, determined by its endowment structure. However, this process is not spontaneous. Without the government playing a facilitating role to overcome inherent coordination and externality problems in the process, the private sector may not be willing to diversify into new sectors based on the changes in the structure of the country's endowment. The RFI concept can help connect resource extraction with the construction of "bottleneck-releasing" infrastructure—two otherwise segregated supply chains, thereby reducing transaction costs.

Second, on the "valuation" issue of the RFI approach, the authors indicate that, ideally, "an RFI credit may be the **least-cost option** for obtaining essential infrastructure that cannot generate sufficient revenue to support a project finance transaction." They also rightly point to gaps left by the previous infrastructural financing models, which could be filled by the RFI approach, including the interesting feature of "nonrecourse" loans. If past RFI deals had indeed included an element of "nonrecourse" loans favoring the borrower, the lender would have assumed higher risks than in the case of full-recourse secured loans. This unique insurance service provided by the lenders in RFI deals, that would otherwise be unavailable, has yet to be fully appreciated and priced-in by the development community. We will leave this issue to further investigation.

Third, the RFI concept helps overcome several constraints in low-income and resource-rich countries, and one of those constraints is the currency mismatch. It is well known that the revenue stream from a specific infrastructure denominated in local currency cannot be used to repay loans denominated in foreign exchange. Ideally, structural transformation should not be constrained by insufficient foreign exchange. The RFI development financing approach focuses on the real sector and relies less on cash flows denominated in foreign exchange. This concept reduces the amount of foreign exchange a country has to have for repayments of foreign debts, as long as it has the potential to produce some commodity that can be sold in the international market such as oil or gas or cocoa beans (in the case of Bui Dam in Ghana) that can generate a revenue stream in the future.

Not all countries have equal access to the international financial market, allowing them to issue bonds for infrastructural development, thus innovative approaches must be found to finance their development. The RFI model allows the exchange of one resource for another productive asset in the long term, and thus supports real sector diversification without relying completely on the financial market. In addition, it reduces the leakages due to resource rents/revenues being transferred out of the country, or capital flight. This "real"-for-"real" sector exchange could help overcome severe financial and governance constraints suffered by low-income but resource-rich countries. For countries constrained by capacity gaps, a "real"-for-"real" exchange, for example, "work for food" programs, turnkey projects, "market for technology" exchanges as well as the "resources for infrastructure" approach, if well designed and monitored, can lead to development results such as roads or schools or jobs on the ground within a time span of three to five years or less.

Fourth, not all asset classes are equal in terms of productivity and their impact on poverty. Some are public- or semi-public goods and others private goods. Certain types of infrastructure are "bottleneck-releasing" with high developmental impact, others are not. The RFI model could help integrate and "bundle" the provision of public goods together with the extraction of natural resources (private goods) in a meaningful way (for example, around an eco-industrial zone) that could benefit the host-country population, as well as making the provision of public goods attractive to the private sector.

What kind of infrastructure investment may "pay for itself" and be financially viable? Here, the economic geography comes into play—infrastructure combined with "cluster-based" industrial zones or urban development can have a bigger impact on growth and poverty. Paul Krugman and other proponents of the new trade theory and the new economic geography have shown that there is a self-reinforcing character to spatial concentration. Business concentration takes place and is sustained because spatial concentration itself creates a favorable economic environment that supports further concentration. These agglomeration benefits reduce the individual firm's transaction costs, and increase the competitiveness of a nation's industry, compared with the same industry in other countries at a similar level of development, as argued by Michael Porter.

Fifth, it is the responsibility of governments and international financial organizations to promote the innovation of contractual arrangements that can turn short-term to long-term financing, nontradables to tradables (as in the case of carbon trade), and illiquid assets to liquid ones (exchange traded funds and asset-based securities). Here, the pooling of risks comes into play. If a Global Structural Transformation Fund (GSTF) that is large enough—at least $50 billion to $100 billion in size and with a diversified portfolio—can be established (Lin and Wang 2013), the risks in bilateral infrastructure projects can be greatly reduced.

Meanwhile, the political economy dimension is critical for risk management. On the one hand, the RFI concept may be welcomed by democratically elected governments, thanks to its ability to "rapidly" achieve developmental results. On the other hand, this feature may be detrimental to the repayment cycle because the next government, having forgotten the benefits obtained in the earlier period, may revoke the concessions or request a renegotiation. In a sample of 1,000 concessions granted by Latin American and Caribbean countries between 1985 and 2000, 30 percent were renegotiated within 2.2 years, with the highest rate of renegotiation being in water and sanitation (74 percent) (Guasch 2004, 12).

There are legitimate concerns over the transparency issues around past RFI packages. We are strongly supportive of the Extractive Industries Transparency Initiative (EITI) principles for moral, political, as well as risk management reasons. History has shown that for political risk management, it is important to keep a balance between the commitment to transparency and a certain level of confidentiality during negotiations (see box 5.4). In our view, **any "deals" negotiated in the dark—without the support of the general public—are more likely to be revoked or renegotiated** later if there is a change in the government. This lesson from history should be kept in mind.

Finally, to the policy makers in Africa who are motivated to build infrastructure for their citizens, this could pay off handsomely if they can carefully identify sectors that are consistent with local comparative advantages and proactively adopt a **cluster-based industrial zone** approach. As China's labor costs rise rapidly, it alone may provide 85 million manufacturing jobs in labor-intensive industries to many low-income countries. One vivid example is Huajian, one of China's largest shoe exporters, which established a large facility in Ethiopia, trained workers, and started exporting within the time span of four months. This factory now employs over 2,000 Ethiopian workers. Huajian could not have achieved this result without the Oriental Industrial Zone jointly developed by the Ethiopian and Chinese governments.

Broadly, establishing a GSTF that closes the infrastructure financing gap will be a "win-win" for the world as well (Lin and Wang 2013). The RFI concept is no panacea as it is only one of several types of infrastructure-financing models, the success of which depends on proper structuring and implementation. Now is the time to put these ideas into practice and build "bottleneck-releasing" infra-structure associated with a country's comparative advantages, urgently needed to support jobs and sustainable growth in both high-income and developing countries.

Note

1. The authors thank Håvard Halland, Bryan Land, Vivien Foster, and Shuilin Wang for discussion. The views expressed here are entirely those of the authors and do not represent the views of the institutions they are affiliated with. Comments and suggestions can be sent to correspondent author Yan Wang at yanwang2@gwu.edu.

Comments by Clare Short

Chair, Extractive Industries Transparency Initiative

The study is a timely contribution to the debate regarding resource financed infrastructure (RFI). The Extractive Industries Transparency Initiative (EITI; www.eiti.org) is based on the principle that a public understanding of government revenues and expenditure can contribute to public debate and inform choice of appropriate and realistic options for sustainable development. This principle is particularly relevant to RFI.

Thirty-nine countries are currently implementing the EITI. In order to achieve compliant status, they are required to publish annual reports that provide timely, comprehensive, and reliable data on the oil, gas, and mining industries. In 2011, the EITI introduced a requirement regarding infrastructure provision and barter arrangements. Where material, EITI implementing countries were required to develop a reporting process "with a view to achieving a level of transparency commensurate with other payments and revenue streams" (EITI Rules, requirement 9(f)). RFI deals were not being singled out or given special treatment. Rather, the EITI board was reiterating the importance of a level playing field, and that the same levels of transparency should apply to all contractual arrangements for resource extraction. In May 2013, the EITI adopted a revised EITI Standard, bringing further clarity to the treatment of what the EITI describes as infrastructure provisions or barter arrangements (see box A.1).

Box A.1 The EITI Standard's Treatment of Resource Financed Infrastructure

Requirement 4.1(d) Infrastructure provisions and barter arrangements
The multistakeholder group and the Independent Administrator are required to consider whether there are any agreements, or sets of agreements, involving the provision of goods and services (including loans, grants, and infrastructure works), in full or partial exchange for oil, gas, or mining exploration or production concessions or physical delivery of such commodities. To be able to do so, the multistakeholder group and the Independent Administrator need to gain a full understanding of the terms of the relevant agreements and contracts,

box continues next page

Box A.1 The EITI Standard's Treatment of Resource Financed Infrastructure (*continued*)

the parties involved, the resources which have been pledged by the state, the value of the balancing benefit stream (for example, infrastructure works), and the materiality of these agreements relative to conventional contracts. Where the multistakeholder group concludes that these agreements are material, the multistakeholder group and the Independent Administrator are required to ensure that the EITI Report addresses these agreements, providing a level of detail and transparency commensurate with the disclosure and reconciliation of other payments and revenues streams. Where reconciliation of key transactions is not feasible, the multistakeholder group should agree on an approach for unilateral disclosure by the parties to the agreement(s) to be included in the EITI Report.

Source: EITI Standard, p. 27.

A central feature of the EITI is the collaboration between government, extractive industry companies, and civil society. In order to address infrastructure provisions and barter arrangements effectively, the EITI requires that stakeholders are able to gain a full understanding of the terms of the relevant agreements and contracts, the parties involved, the resources which have been pledged by the state, the value of the balancing benefit stream (for example, infrastructure works), and the materiality of these agreements relative to conventional contracts.

The EITI Standard also encourages EITI implementing countries to make contracts that provide the terms attached to the exploitation of oil, gas, and minerals public (EITI Requirement 3.12). The EITI Standard goes on to state that "It is a requirement that the EITI Report documents the government's policy on disclosure of contracts…" (EITI requirement 3.12(b)). Contracts in this regard include those involving RFI, subject to the condition that resource exploitation is at least part of a wider RFI. In addition to encouraging the publishing of these arrangements, the consequences of these provisions are that if the government decides not to publish them, it has to explain why in the EITI report. The EITI standard is therefore reflecting the important evolution toward a situation where it is expected that RFI deals are made public.

An early example of how these issues are being addressed in the context of the EITI is the work being done in the Democratic Republic of the Congo (DRC). The most recent EITI Report from the DRC covering fiscal year 2010 provides an overview of an agreement struck in 2007 between the government, through state-owned Gecamines, and a consortium of Chinese companies. The EITI Report also provided details regarding the signature bonuses paid to the government related to this agreement. The EITI Board has welcomed the DRC's initial efforts to address infrastructure provision and barter arrangements, and reiterated that a comprehensive treatment of such deals is necessary in order to meet EITI requirements. There is clearly significant scope to use the EITI platform to increase public awareness about RFI deals, and to provide updates on the implementation of these agreements.

As discussed in the study, a particular challenge with RFI is that it can be difficult to establish reliable estimates of the foregone revenue and the value of the infrastructure to be provided. The costs and benefits may be incurred over long periods, and stakeholders may reasonably disagree on the assumptions that need to be made to estimate their net present value (as, thus, the overall fairness of the deal). Where these agreements are in force, the EITI focuses on providing timely information on the status of the agreements, which allows stakeholders to monitor their implementation and assess their effectiveness.

The study provides useful guidance for how governments can assure good governance and transparency when resource extraction is used to finance infrastructure development. It provides policy makers, contracting parties, and affected communities with a framework for understanding and comparing RFI deals, monitoring their implementation, and assessing both opportunities and risks.

The EITI cannot ensure that natural resource wealth benefits all citizens; this requires a range of broader reform efforts. However, the transparency that the EITI provides can play a key role in informing public debate and stimulating reform.

Comments by Louis T. Wells

Herbert F. Johnson Professor Emeritus, Harvard Business School

"Resource Financed Infrastructure: Origins and Issues" provides a framework for looking at what the authors call resource financed infrastructure (RFI).[1] The title of the study suggests its focus: how to finance infrastructure. One might instead view the arrangements as a result, primarily, of attempts by host countries to obtain the maximum return from the development of their natural resources. In my limited experience, proposals for RFI (whether one reads the term as "resourced financed infrastructure" or "resources for infrastructure") do not usually come to host governments as the result of searches by those governments for ways to finance particular infrastructure projects. So far, I have not seen a government say: "We need a new airport; let's try to finance it by making a deal for access to our iron ore." That day may be arriving, but so far most proposals probably originate from firms seeking to develop mines, oil fields, or plantations. A foreign investor interested in securing resources proposes package deals, RFI deals, as a way to compete for those resources. The host government then has to evaluate the proposals in light of what it might receive otherwise for its resources and what it would pay to finance the associated infrastructure, if it were to proceed with using funds from other sources.[2]

Equivalent to Loans

Regardless of its focus, the study correctly treats RFI as the equivalent of loans secured by pledged resources, whatever the formal structure. Both money from a conventional loan and infrastructure now based on resources extracted in the future yield current assets for a country and require some kind of reimbursement in the future. Either way, they are effectively loans. Well-chosen and carefully developed infrastructure projects, whether paid for by a conventional loan or pledged resources, will generate income for the country that compensates for future debt service. To be sure, if the assets received initially are not wisely invested—for example, if they end up in foreign bank accounts, in white elephant projects, or simply in increased consumption—the country will not generate the increased future income to service the debt. This is the case regardless of how the investment is financed. One can hope, at least, that RFI increases the chances that funds from natural resources will be invested in income-producing assets (useful infrastructure) rather than squandered on foreign bank accounts of officials or spent entirely on current consumption.

Although the focus of analysis may in the end not matter much, the study's emphasis makes RFI look like something new, although the authors do qualify their view on novelty. If one focuses on the goal of obtaining early returns on natural resources, parallel arrangements have been around for a long time. In 1926, Liberia, for example, struck a deal with Firestone for a rubber concession that was accompanied by a loan to the government. True, the proceeds of that loan were not used for infrastructure, but the basic characteristics are similar. Parallel arrangements—assets now for access to minerals or other natural resources— commonly appear in the form of signature bonuses associated with mining and, especially, petroleum agreements. All provide immediate funds to the host country in exchange for rights to natural resources in the future. "Repayment" may be explicit, as can be the case for RFI that diverts, or pledges, revenue from tax or royalty payments to the lender in the future. Or part of the debt service may be less apparent, in the form of lower royalties and taxes paid by the resource developer in order to attract the loan.

RFI deals do differ from simpler loans in that they may be "off book." They can be structured in a way that they do not appear in usual reports of a country's sovereign debt. In this, they have their parallels in off-balance sheet financing raised by companies. Both pose risks, for lenders and borrowers.

Criticisms

RFI deals offered by foreign investors in Africa have been widely criticized, particularly by Western firms and occasionally by Western governments and international organizations. One can understand that Western investors are not enthusiastic about increased competition. Moreover, they may believe (perhaps correctly) that Chinese firms, the firms most frequently involved in such deals, have an advantage in the form of cheap capital and home-government backing that Western firms cannot match. But it is hard to conclude that increased competition is bad for host countries, whether they accept the RFI arrangements or not. Moreover, host countries can only benefit from lower-cost capital, if those lower costs are actually passed on to the host country.

Objections sometimes seem to be about corruption that is said to be involved in such agreements. But there is no evidence, I have seen, that firmly supports the conclusion that RFI deals are associated with more corruption than other natural resource and construction contracts in the same host countries.

Most criticisms levied against RFI, as the authors note, apply equally to independent development of infrastructure and natural resource projects. Conventionally financed infrastructure can also be poorly designed, plagued by corruption, poorly supervised during construction, and not well maintained. Similarly, natural resource agreements are often poorly thought through, full of loopholes, inappropriately designed for community and other local development, and carelessly administered in terms of revenue collection and environmental protection. Poor countries are usually not only poor in terms of per capita gross domestic product (GDP) but also weak in their ability to negotiate with skilled foreign investors and to enforce agreements they have concluded. That is inherent in development and a problem to address, independent of RFI.

Similarly, critics emphasize the secrecy that surrounds most RFI. More transparency would certainly be useful for researchers and, most likely, for host countries. On the other side, arguments put forward by investors for secrecy rarely hold water. But lack of transparency characterizes the bulk of natural resource agreements, whether they involve infrastructure or not.[3]

Risks Down the Road

I do believe that RFI raises another issue that has not been widely recognized or addressed, in the study or elsewhere. If history serves as a guide, RFI deals are especially likely to show up as candidates for renegotiation in the future. To the extent that servicing the debt owed for infrastructure is viewed as reducing government receipts from natural resources, some future government—or government opposition—is very likely to see natural resources being extracted and shipped abroad with fewer net government receipts than what other countries are paid. Except for investors, everyone—but especially political opposition or a new government—is likely to forget the fact that benefits were received early, in the form of infrastructure. Focus turns to the costs. The result of such views, if they do emerge, is pressure to renegotiate.

There was a time when the resulting renegotiations might have upset investors, but might not have created major issues for host countries.[4] They occurred rather frequently, as old bargains seemed to obsolesce.[5] Today, however, with more accessible and enforceable international arbitration, renegotiations can be much more costly to countries than in the past. Governments that are aware of the potential costs of renegotiating with a resistant investor might be hesitant, even in the face of political pressure, to renegotiate. And those who are not so aware end up with high costs of arbitration, if the investor chooses the arbitration route. Neither the frustration of internal political pressures nor the costs of arbitration—in terms of legal fees, awards, and possible damage to the reputation of the country—is minor in terms of the host country's interests.

At least an intuitive understanding of what might happen down the road may underlie some of the reluctance of Western investors to take up the RFI models.

Good or Bad?

Like the authors of "Resource Financed Infrastructure," I believe that RFI models are inherently neither good nor bad for host countries. They should be evaluated like any other business arrangement, and carefully compared to alternative ways of obtaining returns from natural resources or financing infrastructure. Less

Resource Financed Infrastructure • http://dx.doi.org/10.1596/978-1-4648-0239-3

secrecy would lead to easier analysis and comparison of RFI deals, traditional natural resource agreements, and infrastructure finance. Until more data are in the public domain, it is difficult to draw broad generalizations. Yet, the authors provide useful ways to think about individual proposals.

Notes

1. The authors refer to a very useful complementary study: "Building Bridges: China's Growing Role as Infrastructure Financier for Africa: Trends and Policy Options" (Foster and others 2009).

2. Since offers may specify the particular infrastructure project on offer, the government has to ask whether it is a project it would otherwise develop. If the answer is "no," or "only with a low priority," the analysis has to be adjusted for this fact.

3. Note that Liberia has committed to making all its resource agreements public, and published them on the Web. I have seen no evidence that any investor has been harmed by this.

4. In 1975, my coauthor, David N. Smith, and I gave our book, *Negotiating Third World Mineral Agreements*, the subtitle, *Promises as Prologue*, in recognition of the fact that terms of natural resource agreements were constantly renegotiated, in spite of long-lasting commitments seemingly made by both parties. See Smith and Wells (1975).

5. See Vernon (1971, chapter 2) for an early application of the "obsolescing bargain model" to natural resources.

Bibliography

African Mining Vision. 2011. "Exploiting Natural Resources for Financing Infrastructure Development: Policy Options for Africa." African Union Commission. Paper presented at the 2nd Ordinary Session of AU Conference of Ministers Responsible for Mineral Resources Development, Addis Ababa, December.

Alves, Ana Christina. 2013. "China's 'Win-Win' Cooperation: Unpacking the Impact of Infrastructure-for-Resources Deals in Africa." *South African Journal of International Affairs* 20 (2): 207–26.

Brahmbhatt, Milan, and Otaviano Canuto. 2013. "FDI in Least Developed Countries: Problems of Excess?" *Global Finance Mauritius* 1: 79–82.

Brautigam, Deborah. 2011. *The Dragon's Gift: The Real Story of China in Africa*. Oxford: Oxford University Press.

Brealey, Richard A., Ian A. Cooper, and Michel A. Habib. 1996. "Using Project Finance to Fund Infrastructure Investments." *Journal of Applied Corporate Finance* 9 (3): 25-38.

Cassel, Cosima, Giuseppe de Candia, and Antonella Liberatore. 2010. *Building African Infrastructure with Chinese Money*. Barcelona Graduate School of Economics. http://www.barcelonagse.eu/tmp/pdf/ITFD10Africa.pdf.

Dailami, Mansoor, and Danny Leipziger. 1999. *Infrastructure Project Finance and Capital Flows: A New Perspective*. Washington, DC: Economic Development Institute, World Bank.

Davies, Martyn. 2009. "The New Coupling." *Emerging Markets*, May 10. http://www.emergingmarkets.org/Article/2346316/The-new-coupling.html.

Democratic Republic of Congo-Company Corporation Sinohydro, January 2008.

Foster, Vivien. 2008. *Overhauling the Engine of Growth: Infrastructure in Africa* (draft). Washington, DC: World Bank.

Foster, Vivien, and Cecilia Briceño-Garmendia. 2010. *Africa's Infrastructure: A Time for Transformation*. Washington, DC: World Bank.

Foster, Vivien, William Butterfield, Chuan Chen, and Nataliya Pushak. 2009. "Building Bridges: China's Growing Role as Infrastructure Financier for Africa." Trends and Policy Options No. 5, World Bank and PPIAF, Washington, DC.

Freshfields Bruckhaus Deringer. 2012. *From Policy to Proof of Concept, and Beyond: Outlook for Infrastructure 2012*. http://www.freshfields.com/uploadedFiles/SiteWide/News_Room/Insight/Project_Bonds/Outlook%20for%20infrastructure%202012.pdf.

Guasch, J. Luis. 2004. *Granting and Renegotiating Infrastructure Concessions: Doing It Right*. Washington, DC: World Bank.

Global Witness. 2011a. "$6bn Congo-China Resource Deal Threatened by Lack of Information." March 8. http://www.globalwitness.org/library/6bn-congo-china-resource-deal-threatened-lack-information.

———. 2011b. "China and Congo: Friends in Need." A report by Global Witness on the Democratic Republic of Congo, London, United Kingdom.

Group Gecamines-Consortium of Chinese Enterprises. December 2007. Joint Venture Agreement.

Hellendorff, Bruno. 2011. *China and DRC: Africa's Next Top Models?* Chaire InBev Baillet-Latour. https://www.uclouvain.be/cps/ucl/doc/pols/documents/NA13-INBEV-ALL.pdf.

Hodges, John T., and Georgina Dellacha. 2007. "Unsolicited Infrastructure Proposals: How Some Countries Introduce Competition and Transparency." PPIAF Working Paper No. 1, Public-Private Infrastructure Advisory Facility, Washington, DC.

IMF (International Monetary Fund). 2003. "Assessing Public Sector Borrowing Collateralized on Future Flow Receivables." Unpublished memo. https://www.imf.org/external/np/fad/2003/061103.pdf.

Jansson, Johanna. 2011. "The Sicomines Agreement: Change and Continuity in the Democratic Republic of Congo's International Relations." SAIIA Occasional Paper No 97, South African Institute of International Affairs, Johannesburg.

Korea Eximbank. 2011. "Resource Development in DR Congo through Water Supply Pipeline Construction." Press release. http://www.koreaexim.go.kr/en/bbs/noti/view.jsp?no=9671&bbs_code_id=1316753474007&bbs_code_tp=BBS_2.

Lee, Peter. 2010. "China Has a Congo Copper Headache." *Asia Times*, March 11. http://www.atimes.com/atimes/China_Business/LC11Cb02.html.

Lin, Justin Yifu. 2011. "How to Seize the 85 Million Jobs Bonanza." *Let's Talk Development* (blog), World Bank, Washington, DC, July 27.

———. 2012. *New Structural Economics: A Framework for Rethinking Development and Policy.* Washington, DC: World Bank.

Lin, Justin Yifu, and Yan Wang. 2013. "Beyond the Marshall Plan: A Global Structural Transformation Fund." Background paper published by the UN High Level Panel on the Post-2015 Development Agenda. http://www.post2015hlp.org/wp-content/uploads/2013/05/Lin-Wang_Beyond-the-Marshall-Plan-A-Global-Structural-Transformation-Fund.pdf.

Mineral Resources Mining SPRI-National Society of Railways of Congo SARL. 2012. Memorandum of Agreement, June.

Ogier, Thierry. 2011. "Concerns over China's 'Asymmetric Bargaining Power'." *Emerging Markets*, September 24. http://www.emergingmarkets.org/Article/2906476/Concerns-over-Chinas-asymmetric-bargaining-power.html.

Ravat, Anwar, and Sridar P. Kannan, eds. 2011. *Implementing EITI for Impact: A Handbook for Policy Makers and Stakeholders.* Washington, DC: World Bank.

Smith, David N., and Louis T. Wells. 1975. *Negotiating Third World Mineral Agreements.* Cambridge, MA: Ballinger.

Society of Industrial and Mining Development of Congo SARL-Tae Joo Synthesis Steel Co., Ltd. 2011. Operating Agreement, March.

UNCTAD (United Nations Conference on Trade and Development). 2013. "Time Series on Inward and Outward Foreign Direct Investment Flows, Annual, 1970–2012." Data Compiled by the *Financial Times* August 19, 2013, "Offshore Centres Race to Seal Africa Investment Tax Deals." http://www.ft.com/intl/cms/s/0/64368e44-08c8-11e3-ad07-00144feabdc0.html.

Vernon, Raymond. 1971. *Sovereignty at Bay*. New York: Basic Books.

Wang, Yan. 2011. "Infrastructure: The Foundation for Growth and Poverty Reduction: A Synthesis." In *Economic Transformation and Poverty Reduction: How It Happened in China, Helping It Happen in Africa*, edited by China-OECD/DAC Study Group, chapter III, volume II. OECD and International Poverty Reduction Center in China. http://www.oecd.org/dac/povertyreduction/49528657.pdf.

Wells, Louis T. 2013. "Infrastructure for Ore: Benefits and Costs of a Not-So-Original Idea." Columbia FDI Perspectives, No. 96, June 3. http://www.vcc.columbia.edu/content/infrastructure-ore-benefits-and-costs-not-so-original-idea.

Wenping, He. 2012. "Laying Foundation for Future." *China Daily*, June 29. http://usa.chinadaily.com.cn/weekly/2012-06-29/content_15534111.htm.

Environmental Benefits Statement

The World Bank is committed to reducing its environmental footprint. In support of this commitment, the Publishing and Knowledge Division leverages electronic publishing options and print-on-demand technology, which is located in regional hubs worldwide. Together, these initiatives enable print runs to be lowered and shipping distances decreased, resulting in reduced paper consumption, chemical use, greenhouse gas emissions, and waste.

The Publishing and Knowledge Division follows the recommended standards for paper use set by the Green Press Initiative. Whenever possible, books are printed on 50 percent to 100 percent postconsumer recycled paper, and at least 50 percent of the fiber in our book paper is either unbleached or bleached using Totally Chlorine Free (TCF), Processed Chlorine Free (PCF), or Enhanced Elemental Chlorine Free (EECF) processes.

More information about the Bank's environmental philosophy can be found at http://crinfo.worldbank.org/wbcrinfo/node/4.

green
press
INITIATIVE

www.ingramcontent.com/pod-product-compliance
Lightning Source LLC
Chambersburg PA
CBHW080001280326
41935CB00013B/1707